A Guide to Interpersonal Communication: Student Handbook 2006~2007

Lisa Sparks, Ph.D.
Chapman University

Don Boileau, Ph.D.
&
Brigit Keelin Talkington, M. A.
Department of Communication
George Mason University

Bent Tree Press
Introduction to Interpersonal Communication
Course # COMM 101
GEORGE MASON UNIVERSITY
Instructors: Lisa Sparks, Ph.D., Chapman University
Don Boileau, Ph.D., & Brigit Keelin Talkington M. A., George Mason University
ISBN: 1-933005-63-7

The development of this course and handbook has evolved for more than 10 years and has been influenced by many great scholars, educators, and friends. I am especially appreciative of the conceptual and creative contributions made by the faculty at George Mason University who helped to develop the conceptual framework for the presenting with technology course. Appreciation and acknowledgement is also given to the students who have contributed their speeches and outlines, and to those who graciously helped in the creation of many of the assignments and activities from my early graduate school days at University of Oklahoma to time spent with students at University of Texas-San Antonio and especially George Mason University. Special thanks go to the creative contributions of Dr. Christine Smith, Dr. Sheryl Friedley, Dr. Janette Muir, Dr. Joani Bedore, Maria Chilcote, Annika Hylmo, Lucy Holsenbake, Brigitte Hinkle, Barra Kahn, Ray McKelvy, Laura Wheeler Poms, Terri Wray, and GMU adjunct faculty for their thoughtful improvements over the last several years.

All proceeds from this publication are paid directly to the George Mason University Foundation for support of the Basic Course Program within the Communication Department.

Printed in the United States of America.

ISBN: 1-933005-63-7

Bent Tree Press

59 Damonte Ranch Parkway, Suite B284 ● Reno, NV 89521 ● (800) 970-1883

www.benttreepress.com

Address all correspondence and order information to the above address.

Table of Contents

A Guide to Interpersonal Communication: Student Handbook

Syllabus and Assignments

Syllabus ~ COMM 101

Course Description:

Students will learn the skills and strategies used in interpersonal and small group communication situations. This course introduces students to the principles involved in communicating in interpersonal relationships and small groups.

Course Objective/Rationale:

During the course you will write about concepts in the text that relate to your everyday lives; observe group interaction processes while participating in face-to-face groups; practice group problem-solving by devising and facilitating a solution to a problem ; analyze relationships in a film and write about observed relationships; conduct an interview assignment. In this course, you will be asked to present two oral reports. It is important that you develop your interpersonal communication skills and that you learn how to present analyses of interpersonal and small group relationships. The goal is for you to gain more confidence in interpersonal and small group communicative settings.

Instructor: _____ **Voicemail: 703-993-1090 /** _____

Office: _____ **Office Hours:**_____

E-mail: _____

Preferred method of contacting your instructor: _____

Required Textbooks:
Wood, J. T. (2006). *Interpersonal communication: An introduction to the field of communication, 4e.* Belmont, CA: Wadsworth/Thomson Learning.

Sparks, L., Boileau, D., & Talkington, B. K. (2006). *A guide to interpersonal communication: Student handbook, 2006-2007.* Reno, NV: Bent Tree Press.

Student Learning Objectives:

Oral communication competency at George Mason University is defined as the ability to use oral communication as a way of thinking and learning as well as sharing ideas with others. The general education program identifies numerous learning goals in oral communication, which are addressed specifically in two Communication courses, COMM 100, Public Speaking and COMM 101, Interpersonal and Group Interaction. Common to both courses are these six learning goals:
1. Students will understand the role of free speech in a democratic society.
2. Students will learn and practice principles of ethical communication.
3. Students will understand the influence of culture in communication and will know how to cope with cultural differences when presenting information to an audience.
4. Students will develop analytical skills and critical listening skills.
5. Students will understand and practice effective elements of verbal and nonverbal communication.
6. Students will demonstrate understanding of and proficiency in constructing multiple message types.

Goals for COMM 101, Interpersonal and Group Interaction:

1. Students will critically analyze and synthesize interpersonal communication research by gaining an understanding of the concepts, principles, and theories of interpersonal communication.
2. Students will develop specific skills that enhance the interpersonal communication process and that demonstrate understanding of the influence of perception and cultural factors in interpersonal communication.
3. Students will assess the influence of communication climate and multiple contexts on their own interpersonal communication.
4. Students will understand the interrelationship between interpersonal concepts and the small group process by acquiring problem-solving skills through experiential learning and through working in small groups and teams.
5. Students will learn and practice the principles and techniques of effective oral communication by producing individual and group presentations.

Course Requirements:

PARTICIPATION:

ATTENDANCE: Following University policy, I EXPECT you to be in class. The only excused absences are for 1) illness; 2) compelling circumstances beyond your control; 3) religious observances, or 4) participation in University activities at the request of an authority of the University. I will note any and all absences. If you want to request credit for a particular absence (i.e. for full assignment credit, not participation credit) you must notify me in writing and with appropriate documentation no later than two weeks after the absence. Excessive absences will likely result in lower grades from missed/late work, missed quizzes, and uncovered classroom material as well as from a possible reduction in participation credit. *Again: you are responsible for material covered in class whether you are present or not.*

TIMELINESS: Late arrivals receive less participation credit, as do those who leave class early. I will ask those who are excessively tardy to leave the classroom for creating a classroom distraction.

Make every effort to inform me if an emergency prevents you from giving a presentation on an assigned date. If you miss, or are late for, your scheduled presentation time a grade penalty of 10 percent is automatically imposed and will increase by 10% every class meeting thereafter. No exceptions.

> **It is critical that you stay in touch with me by phone or e-mail when you are experiencing illness or difficulty. If you wait until your problems are over to talk to me, I may have no option but to fail you based on course policies. This is a communication course, communicate to me to discuss options.**

Exams:
Two multiple-choice exams will be given. Bring a pencil and Scantron sheet to each exam (get Scantrons at the GMU bookstore by the checkout stand). Each exam will emphasize readings from the text and material covered in class. The first exam is worth 150 points and will cover chapters 1-6. The final exam is worth 200 points; it will be comprehensive (i.e., include elements from every chapter in the book). Approximately 70 percent of the final exam will cover chapters 7-12, and the Appendix. Approximately 30 percent of the final will be taken from material covered on the first exam. Your instructor may or may not conduct a review and/or provide a review study guide. Such reviews may be detrimental to student performance because students fail to review all course materials. Additionally, remedial work or review activities take away from instructional time that is better used for further exploration of course material. Reviews are best conducted in ongoing small groups outside of class. This process of reviewing with fellow classmates is highly recommended.

Exam makeup policy: Missing an exam without prior and proper notification of your instructor will result in an **automatic grade reduction of 10 percent per day.** You must make up a missed exam within 1 week, and if necessary arrange to have the exam proctored by another faculty member in order to meet that deadline. After 1 week, a grade of "0" is assigned. No exceptions.

Prearranged alternative exam date policy: Any requests to take the exam on a date other than the date specified must be made at least a month in advance and are granted solely at my discretion. Making arrangements, such as having your exam proctored by another faculty member, or taking your exam with another section, is your responsibility, however, **you must make sure both instructors are aware of arrangements in advance. Note: Final exam policy is different. Prior approval from the Dean may be required to take your final exam at an alternative time. It is your responsibility to get approval.**

Going over exams: I will go over the questions most frequently missed by your class. If you would like to view your exam, you must arrange to do so during my office hours. You are not allowed to keep or make notes from the exam.

Written Assignments:
All written assignments are to be printed and turned in with the correct grading sheet attached. As you create documents (and slides), save ALL your files using this naming format:

Material turned in later than class time: The following is my late policy:

_____

_____

_____

_____

Remember to save all assignments done on your computer. This habit is a good one for all your classes while at George Mason University. Such practices have advantages if a paper is lost or at the end of the semester you are involved in a grade complaint.

Research requirement:
Research is critical to the generation of new knowledge, and understanding of the research process is one of the primary goals of a University education. Your participation in research, therefore, is essential and some of your grade will reflect your participation. Activities may include coding data, filling out a survey, engaging in role-playing or group work, or other research-related procedures. Participation in a given project must be approved by me for credit to be given. I will notify you of specific research opportunities.

Grades:
You will be graded in this class based on the number of points you earn for each exam, speech, written assignment or other activity, as well as your class participation. The total number of points available for the semester is 1000. Keep track of your scores on the Student's Record of Grades form. At semester's end, add up your points and use the chart provided below. If you have any questions concerning GMU grading policies call the Assistant Registrar for academic records 703-993-2462 or the academic records staff 703-993-2435.

A+	97-100 (970-1000)
A	93-96 (930-969)
A-	90-92 (900-929)
B+	87-89 (870-899)
B	83-86 (830-869)
B-	80-82 (800-829)
C+	77-79 (770-799)
C	70-76 (730-769)
D	60-69 (600-699)
F	59 or less (599 or less)

Student notification of grades:
Grade reports are not automatically mailed to students at the end of the term. Instead, students may access their grades by logging onto: *https://patriotweb.gmu.edu* Usually your grade will be posted within 3 business days of your final exam.

*NOTE: It is helpful to keep track of your grades on the sheet provided in this Handbook. You can then determine your grade at any time during the semester by adding up your scores and dividing that total by the total number of points possible for the graded work. **As in all 100 and 200 level courses, a midterm grade will be posted. If you are concerned please check with your instructor.**

Posting grades publicly:
The posting of student grades by student name or ID number---at any time, in any format---is not allowed at GMU. This policy has been in effect since May 1990 to comply with the Family Educational Rights and Privacy Act of 1974 (FERPA), as amended.

Special Notes:

Academic Misconduct:
The guidelines in the <u>Student Code of Responsibility and Conduct for GMU</u> will be upheld in this course. According to the Academic Misconduct Code:

> *Academic misconduct includes (a) cheating (using unauthorized materials, information, or study aids in any academic exercise, plagiarism, falsification of records, unauthorized possession of examinations, intimidation, any and all other actions that may improperly affect the evaluation of a student's academic performance or achievement); (b) assisting others in any such act; or (c) attempts to engage in such act.*

Academic misconduct will not be tolerated and will be severely penalized, and possibly result in a failing grade for the class. In the event of misconduct, the appropriate dean will be notified and the case handled according to University policy.

Furthermore, we take the GMU Honor Code very seriously. Unless otherwise indicated (as in a group project), all work and discussion is to be your own. Plagiarism is representing another's work as your own or recycling earlier work as new work without consulting the instructor. Digital technologies make it possible to cut and paste work–remember that if you don't cite it, it is plagiarism and you are plagiarizing! Remember to use proper source citations in crediting the evidence, ideas and quotations of others that you use in your work. All quizzes and other assessment measures must be completed on your own with no outside help. Academic dishonesty also includes providing false or misleading information in order to receive a postponement or an extension on tests, quizzes, or assignments. Academic dishonesty, or a failure to follow the GMU Honor Code, will most likely result in a course grade of F and may result in further academic penalties.

Incompletes or Withdrawals:
It is extremely unlikely that an incomplete will be assigned. Students requesting an incomplete must be passing the course, must still complete all of the assignments, quizzes, and exams allowable (not all can be made up if missed), must provide compelling evidence justifying an incomplete, and must sign an incomplete contract with the course instructor. Mid- to late-semester withdrawal requests are evaluated by the Dean's office on a case-by-case basis.

Reasonable Accommodation:
A Disability Support Services office is available on campus to assist students with special needs. If you have a disability or suspect you might have a disability, contact this office at 703-993-2474. If you have a verified disability and will require assistance, let me know within the first two weeks of this course.

The GMU Writing Center:
The Writing Center provides free tutorial sessions for all students needing help with any writing project--from freshman essays to scholarly publications. It is best to make an appointment to ensure seeing a Writing Center consultant at a specific time; however, walk-ins will be accepted if there are openings. The GMU Writing Center is located at UWC: Robinson A114. Phone: 703-993-1200. Web page:
http://writingcenter.gmu.edu/

Useful websites for students, writers, researchers, and educators:
Guide to grammar—this is a very thorough and well-organized site with clear explanations of grammar conventions. Also includes quizzes for those who are looking for a grammar and mechanics challenge.
http://www.ccc.commnet.edu/grammar/

Academic Writing Online---this is an excellent online journal featuring scholarly articles about writing, and writing culture, as well as a link to *Language and Learning in the Discipline's* website.
http://wac.colostate.edu/aw/

What is an "A" paper---this gives students a basic idea of C-based grading scales and criteria for writing well in a variety of disciplines.
http://www.calstatela.edu/centers/write_cn/apaper.htm

Notes and Changes:

Student's Record of Grades

Assignments	Points
Small Group Exercise in Class	_____/50
Oral Presentation as part of the Symposium Assignment	_____/100
Personal Evaluation	_____/50
Conflict Resolution	_____/50
Dyadic Exercise	_____/100
Written	_____/50

Exams

I (Chapters 1-6) (40 questions: multiple choice format + short answer)	_____/150
Final (30% exam I; 70% Chs. 7-12 & Appendix) (40 questions multiple choice format + short answer)	_____/150
Participation Points	_____/100
Instructor Options	_____/100

Possible Options:
Team Workshops & Activities
IP Reflection/Observation
Homework
Research Participation

Subtotal	_____/1000

TOTAL   _____

*NOTE: It is helpful for you to record your grades for this class.

Your instructor will detail his or her schedule of graded assessments during the first week of classes.

Tentative Semester Schedule for COMM 101

Date	Week	Topic	Assignments	Readings
	1	Syllabus/A first look at interpersonal communication The field of communication		Ch. 1
	2	Communication and the Creation of Self Perception and Communication		Ch. 2 Ch. 3
	3	The World of Words		Ch. 4
	4	Interpersonal Communication	Dyadic Exercise	
	5	The World Beyond Words		Ch. 5
	6	Mindful Listening **Dyadic Exercise**		Ch. 6
	7	**MIDTERM EXAM** Set Up Symposium Groups Public Speaking in a Nutshell (Handbook)	Bring Green Scantron	
		Note: you will want to check your midterm grade; if problems, see your instructor.		
	8	Emotions and Communication Symposium Presentation Small Group Communication in a Nutshell (Handbook0	Team # 1	Ch. 7
	9	**Small Group Exercises in Class**	Bring Evaluation Sheets	!
	10	Communication Climate: Personal Relationships Symposium Presentation-		Ch. 8
	11	Managing Conflict in Relationships Symposium Presentation		Ch. 9
	12	Friendships in Our Lives Symposium Presentation	Conflict Exercise	Ch. 10
	13	Committed Romantic Relationships		Ch. 11
	14	Communication in Families		Ch. 12
Date: Place: Time:		**FINAL EXAM ~ is COMPREHENSIVE! Bring Scantron**	FINAL EXAM	

A Guide to Interpersonal Communication: Student Handbook

Readings on Group Communication & Public Speaking

Group Communication in a Nutshell

Don M. Boileau

13

You will make decisions in a small group of people throughout your life. Thus, you will want to ask, "How do I apply what I am learning in interpersonal communication to the small group setting?" Many of the communication skills you are learning will apply directly to the small group situation. Small group communication on a spectrum of audience differences for the communication discipline functions between interpersonal communication [one-on-one] and public speaking [one-to-many] with its communication among a few people.

While one can take many courses in small group communication, we will focus on some of the basic small group principles and skills in this course—principles and skills to form a foundation for better choices by you for the rest of your life. A group might be defined as "three or more people who interact over time, depend upon one another, and follow shared rules of conduct to reach a common goal" (Wood, 2004, p. 257). While groups can have many purposes (focus groups, brainstorming groups, advisory groups, and decision making), we will focus on decision making groups and symposium groups.

Sometimes as a group you will make presentations. The most common format for group presentations is the symposium, which is a small group of people making speeches around a common topic. Each person develops a different idea or perspective about the topic. The symposium format is one of the assignments in this course.

We will focus on discovering on the following fundamentals of small group communication: 1) basic principles of group decision making, 2) the process of group decision making, 3) the responsibilities of group members, 4) the leadership tasks in groups, and 5) the use of interpersonal communication in the group.

1. Basic Principles of Group Decision Making

These principles will overlap because of communication. We have the perspective that oral communication changes the meanings as the group agenda advances. People do make a difference—sometimes major differences and sometimes only in the nuances of meaning that people have. You must remember that each group reflects both the quality and the quantity of communication by the members. George Grice and John Skinner (2007) argue that five principles underlie group discussion and group decision making. As you participate in groups you will discover how each principle operates.

The first principle is that **group decision making is a shared responsibility.** Each member shares the responsibility to help the group achieve its goals. This communication demand is part of each person's responsibility. The most common rationale group members often make for not commenting is "Someone already said something like what I was thinking so why should I add my two-bits." As we are learning in this course, meanings vary among people. Even the same word can have different images in people's minds. The impetus of this principle is to make sure by communication that each member understands what is happening. The nature of leadership that we want you to remember is a concept of completing the leadership functions. Thus, each member has the responsibility to step in when some type of function does not occur.

The second principle is that group **decision making requires an understanding of goals.** A common frustration with having to be in a group is that people often do not know what the group goal is. Thus, a major communication task for a group is to state clearly what the goals are for the group for that particular day. The communication question is "What are our goals for the day?" Or someone may ask the question "What is the purpose of the meeting today?" Too often people begin group decision making tasks without an idea of what the goal is. Thus, a communication task a group gathering is to establish the purpose or goals of the gathering. Many meetings have a printed agenda to help clarify what the initial goals are.

A third principle reminds groups that any agenda needs to be both specific and flexible. Specificity comes from the former principle as a good communication habit of making sure the goals are known. Flexibility also comes from communication, because as the meeting progresses, new ideas and meanings unfold as participants interact. As each person adds a comment to a group, a new meaning is created. Even if the group has to reject the suggestion as irrelevant, someone needs to make that comment. If each person is created to the specific goals of the group, then that agenda needs to be addressed. Its specificity is often developed by the communication in the group. Most times what were the specifics at the start of the meeting have been extended, modified, or changed by the communication in the group.

To respond to other people in a helpful fashion requires a need for open communication—the fourth principle. If everyone thought alike the power of the group would be lost as the input of others would not be needed. Decision making in groups is enhanced by people adding ideas to the conversations in the group. The basic assumption for this principle has been often demonstrated in groups because the decision with more people's ideas added to the discussion is a better decision. To do this people have to discuss the merits of the ideas and not be become involved in personality conflicts.

In order to have constructive ideas in a group, the group needs accurate information, so the fifth principle is that participants need to bring adequate and accurate information to the discussion. If only one or two people do the research, then they will not only dominate, but they will also not have as much information as when all the participants are prepared. In most group situations a division of labor can occur, so that the each person can gather different types of information. Even though some overlap might occur, each person doing two hours of work gives the group ten hours of research on the common problem. Also, each person can contribute to the critical analysis of the data being provided. Such analysis also depends on the principle of open communication so that the group can have the best available information to aid in the decision process.

2. Steps in Problem Solving Problem Discussion

The basic problem solving sequence in most group discussion textbooks comes from the thinking of the American philosopher, John Dewey. He outlined the process in a small book called *How We Think*. These steps start with defining the problem and end with selecting a solution to the problem that was defined.

The first step, and often that many groups ignore until they are floundering, is **to define the problem**. While it is easy to ask "What is the problem we are facing?" it is much harder to define all the facets of the problem. It may seem obvious that one would ask about the problem in a problem solving group, but my own experience is that people often do not want to take the time to define the elements of the problem. People generally want to talk about solutions, especially the one they might be advocating. It requires discipline in the group to stick to defining the problem. By clearly identifying what exactly the problem is the group wants to solve, the group will need to spend less time on other aspects of the sequence. The principle identified above about bringing adequate and accurate information to the discussion particularly applies in defining the problem.

When you have defined the problem a good question to ask is "What factors contribute to the problem?"

The answer to that helps the group start the second step which is to **analyze the problem.** To do this one can also ask "what are the symptoms to the problem." Analysis helps answer the questions of "Why are we having this problem?" and "What are the consequences of this problem?" This step also requires careful study of the problem so that the information provided is accurate and does reflect the problem. Sometimes people like to add information that may not be relevant to the problem, so it is helpful to have defined the problem clearly. Often participants at this stage may start to argue for a specific solution to the problem as they might see the problem in a particular perspective from their own viewpoint. It is important not to start discussing solutions at this stage.

The third step is to then develop a criterion that one might want for any solution to the problem. **The criterion for the optimal solution also takes** time to develop. For some problems the group might want the solution not to cause any increased taxes—a desirable goal until one might ask what programs have to be cut in order to keep that standard. Someone might ask is there another way to raise money for the solution. A discussion like this may lead to a new criterion that limits the tax increase to a certain dollar amount or a certain percentage. One of the powers of group problem solving discussion is that ideas from other often modify our own thinking as the problem is addressed systematically. The goal for the group is to come up with criteria that make sense for the problem under discussion.

Thus, it is not until the fourth step that the group wants to **propose solutions.** Sometimes this step requires that the group practice brainstorming. Brainstorming is the process of adding down every idea that is mentioned without any pre-judging it. No matter how ridiculous a solution is the note-taker of the group writes it down. The goal of the group for this stage is to produce a list of possible solutions. One almost has to forget the previous step of writing down the criteria as often one of those standards will not be met. Rarely will a group come up with a solution that meets all the standards in the criteria. To prevent this self-judging, the group needs to make sure that these two steps of setting the criteria and proposing solutions are clearly separate activities. Each member needs to take on the group task of getting a good list of solutions, even if the emphasis is on producing a good number of solutions rather than just one solution.

When the list of solutions is developed, then the group merges these last two steps and **considers each solution against the criteria already established.** Some groups find it helpful to look at the advantages and disadvantages of each solution. If the note-taker has both the criteria and the various solutions on separate sheets of paper, then it is easy to be systematic for this stage. If a group has worked together for a long time, this stage might go quickly. The danger here is to become a victim of *groupthink* and to let the idea of one person slip through with out systematically examining each solution against the criteria. Groupthink is when the group under the guise of what seems to be an obvious solution agrees to one solution quickly without considering the disadvantages of that solution. People with doubts about the selected solution decide not to voice those doubts. People often use the historical examples of groupthink such as the Bay of Pigs decision or the discussion to go ahead with the Challenger flight when many people had information that should have been used to challenge those decisions. Sometimes this step can be done quickly as it may be apparent that several of the solutions will not come close to the criteria. No matter what the good leader will systematically bring up each solution.

The final step is to **select an option as the solution and implement it.** Most times even a single solution might be divided into what needs to be done immediately and what can be done later. While discussing the selected solution, participants often assign people various tasks. Other groups in this step will develop a time line for implementing the solution. Others will take each task for that solution an assign a single person with the responsibility of getting the task done. Legal and economic implications are discussed in this stage so that people know how the solution will be implemented.

It is not uncommon as one goes through this process to re-cycle back to an earlier stage. Another solution might appear as the selection process narrows down to two alternatives, so that the group might want to combine some of the elements of each. At other times, as discussion progresses it becomes apparent because of financial restraints that the group needs to change the criteria for the solution. This re-cycling only indicates the power of the group in creating a better solution because of the multiple perspectives that different members bring to the group.

3. Responsibilities of Group Members

Besides a basic responsibility to be concerned with leadership tasks mentioned below, each member also needs to be as **effective communicator** as one can be. Three types of comments help develop ones skill as a communicator: 1) comments about the content of the group task, 2) comments about the communication climate and the cohesion of the group, and 3) leadership tasks [which are explained in the next section]

The major task of a participant is **to provide information relevant to the content** of the group. Such comments may be providing original ideas or information relevant to the topic. A group member wants to add to the information available to the group as well as explore what the meaning is of other information—both of these comments are part of the content orientation of the group. For example, if the group was trying to solve a parking problem at GMU, that member might add new information to the group with a comment like, "The cost of each parking spot in the parking garage is over $16,000 when the facility was built." Another member might develop the meaning of such information with a response to that comment with "That would mean that if we depreciated that spot over 30 years, the spot would have to generate over $500 a year in revenue per parking spot." Another member could add to the meaning of the comment by a statement such as, "Then with additional demands for upkeep and operation of the garage, the cost of the spot should exceed at least $600 a year." Then another member might ask the question, "Do people who get reserved spots pay more than $600 a year for that privilege?" Thus, one piece of original information could generate several others adding to that information by both analysis and question asking. Each of the steps mentioned above bring a different type of comment to the group.

Another group of comments are labeled **"climate comments"** as they are not directed to the subject matter under discussion, but address other group members as to their needs and situations. These socio-emotional comments range from general comments, such as "How are you doing, Mary?" to "I may seem to be negative in my comments tonight. I noted my last few comments seemed to attack the person, and not the evidence they were sharing with us." A member might comment, "I am glad to hear your perspective, Abdul." Sometimes members will add a joke to ease the tension rising in the group even though the joke has nothing to do with the topic. Sometimes conflict will break out in a group, and one or more participants will try to bridge the gaps by putting comments which are directed to the people involved.

The third type of comments relate to leadership tasks, which are developed in the next section.

4. Leadership Tasks

While academics debate the relative merits of groups with a leader vs. leaderless groups, the idea we want to convey is learning what the leadership tasks are. These comments focus on the procedural communication necessary to keep the group on task. Often in the business, institutional, and governmental worlds a group will have an appointed leader. But in the voluntary area of clubs, scouts, school groups, churches, interest groups, many groups run without a designated leader. Either way a series of leadership tasks have to be achieved.

The first step is to start the group and make sure everyone understands the purpose of the meeting. Sometimes this task will entail the creation of the agenda and at other times an exploration of what the group wants to accomplish. A strong beginning of the group is important. Some groups will want to start with a type of sharing of experiences which can range from experience with the problem to social concerns for the members. This type of start has an interpersonal goal of recognizing each member of the group as well as helping them by talking. It can also lead to just allowing each person to feel comfortable for talking.

A second task is to **ensure effective participation.** This may require asking members about their reactions to the ideas of others or it may require that one stop someone from dominating the conversation. While an exactly equal participation is almost impossible to reach, it is still important to draw into the discussion various group members. This task is important to help prevent group think form occurring by making sure those with doubts about some of the ideas can express their reservations. While some people think of leaders as having to have the answers, this task indicates that a leadership function is to ask questions of others. It is important to know that in many groups a person may listen without commenting for a long time, only to come up with the best analysis of the situation and to have great ideas about the dimensions of the solution.

The third task is **to keep the group on task.** It is easy for any group to get off task. While some socio-emotional comments are helpful to the group, especially for long term groups, the purpose of the group must be met. The challenge here is to make sure the group has enough time to solve the problem, but on the other hand is not to let each issue be "beat to death" by too many comments.

While keeping the group on task, the fourth leadership function is **to make internal summaries** as to what the group has agreed upon. This communication task helps keep the group systematically going through the steps of the problem solving method. Like making a speech, the communication goal here is to summarize what has been decided and to make sure the group has agreed to it. Sometimes a group will spend time creating a consensus that all can agree upon, and other times a majority of the group will be used to make a decision. Such a decision as to the process needs to be decided upon at the start of the group discussion. Consensus building takes a long time, but has the advantage of all the members buying into the action. Democratic action is typical of our society. For groups it helps to know why people are both for and against the action. By knowing what the opposition to your idea consists of, one can adapt the solution in ways to prevent a disaster from occurring later.

The last leadership task is **to help the group make the decision and then implement it.** This task is the accumulation of the other tasks and then making sure the group discusses how the decision will be accomplished. Often, this task is to decide a) who will do what, b) what resources are needed, c) what time line is necessary, and d) how the solution will be evaluated by the group. It is important that everyone clearly knows what the solution is. Sometimes groups just conclude only to discover disagreement as what the solution is. Thus, a communication task is to make sure the leader announces clearly what was agreed upon during the discussion. This last function helps the group in future discussions by knowing how well they functioned in coming up to a solution. Sometimes barriers the group is worked about do not materialize, and other times some unexpected consequences appear. Whatever happens, this is the way the group can learn about their effectiveness.

5. The use of interpersonal communication

In this class you are learning how verbal and nonverbal communication choices enhance the effectiveness of helping others understand our meanings. We can use our communication skills to help the group function. From what we are learning in the class the following behaviors have been noted by people as helping the group perform better.

Since people have names, the **use of names** not only personalizes the discussion, but it is a way to focus on ideas rather than people. By addressing people by name in a group occasionally [we do not want to overdue the use of names or it sounds artificial] the group atmosphere becomes more personal. If one says, "Aisha's idea of using one of the depreciation methods to figure out the cost would be an effective way to price the parking spot," then the idea ownership of the idea is recognized as well as providing a method for pricing.

The use of **"I" statements** in a dyadic situation has the same positive consequence in the group setting. By placing the personal program at the beginning of the sentence, we shift the direction of the comment from attacking the other person to the placement of one's own reaction. The comment *"What do I think?"* focuses on the reaction to an idea rather than the person having the idea. Thus, "I would hate to have students pay more for parking than administrators" conveys the reaction and the content statement together. This form is better than "That crazy idea of yours has students subsidize the parking garage while administrators don't pay their full share."

Simple **questions** often draw other people into the conversation in a non-threatening manner. It is easy to say, "Amy, what is your reaction to Ariff's idea of calculating the cost of an individual spot before setting the fees?" Then, the way Amy answers provides insight into how to draw her in to participating more throughout the discussion. The goal is **to involve as many members as one can** in the discussion. There is a tendency in groups for people to allow others to dominate the discussion. Questions about content, reaction to the content, the feeling about the group's progress, the participation of others—all are ways to get people to participate.

Another application of interpersonal communication is **a commitment to critical evaluation of the ideas** and not the person. One might say "the weakness of just using depreciation costs of the capital expenditures is that we might not cover the operating costs—a parking garage needs money takers, people to clean it up, people to paint it periodically, and people to do the hiring." Such a sentence does not have a complaint in it about the person who wanted the capital expenditures to be the base line and not the operating costs and the capital expenditures.

Use **paraphrasing skills** to summarize the statements of others. This skill combines what we have learned about listening. By paraphrasing the ideas rather than quote them, one signals to the listeners what you are thinking. This task also relates to the internal summaries needed in leadership tasks. When we interpret what another has said in our own words, we send them the message as to our understanding. This allows the other person to respond to the accuracy of your interpretation.

- -

Note: If you expect to be in a job with many meetings, and many among you will be managers and leaders in organizations, consider taking Comm 201: Small Group Communication to develop your skills in group discussion. If you want to know how communication functions in organizations, consider taking Comm 335: Organizational Communication.

Public Speaking in a Nutshell

Brigit Keelin Talkington

Yes, we know this is for a required class. So, let's make this experience as painless as possible, OK? Public Speaking (rhetoric/oratory) has been studied for a long time. Most books discuss the ancient Greek and Roman periods (Socrates, Plato, Aristotle, Cicero, and Quintilian) as the "golden age" of rhetoric. Obviously, communication happened before then (from the first humans on) and was even studied before then (Old Sea Scrolls, Chinese texts and Egyptian papyrus texts attest to these earlier efforts), but the Greeks and later the Romans were some of the first peoples to study rhetoric and write about it in an official and organized way. It has been studied ever since, in ways both scientific and humanistic. This history gives the communication discipline a strong footing, and is a good place from which to start your studies. This discussion will start out by discussing the five cannons of rhetoric (5 elements of public speaking developed and refined by the aforementioned Greeks and Romans), and then apply those stages to the speech preparation process for your purposes here in the modern day. After that we'll discuss the different options of delivery and some understandings that might help with any nervousness you feel about giving a speech in public.

The five cannons of rhetoric

The textbook you would be using if you were taking Public Speaking is written by Steven and Susan Beebe (Beebe, 2006); they discuss the cannons of rhetoric as separate arts that work together to allow for successful speech creation. The five basics, these cannons, are invention, arrangement, style, memory, and delivery. Here is a very brief description of each as it applies to public speaking.

Invention is getting together your facts and evidence early on in the process, inventing your argument. Arrangement is the organization of your speech – this will be discussed in much more detail below. Style relates to eloquent and effective language use. Memory deals with being able to remember your speech – both for you as a source of communication and for your audience as receivers of communication. Delivery is the polish on the presentation that makes it shine, considering both the words used (verbal) and all the body language and vocal elements that aren't actual word choices (nonverbal). For more on this, see Beebe and Beebe (2006, p. 455), or better yet, sign up for COMM 100 next semester!

The speech preparation process

The speech preparation process is very similar to what you may have been exposed to in a high school English Composition class. You'll find many parallels to English Composition in the speech preparation process. There are also some differences. Those similarities and differences will now be discussed, as will the Introduction, Body and Conclusion of your speech.

You have probably had more experience with written communication classes than oral communication classes. You probably know to compose a paper with an introduction, a body and a conclusion. But what you may not be as familiar with are the similarities and the differences between the oral and the written communication styles. Oral communication style is more informal, simpler and more repetitive than the written communication style. You use more pronouns when speaking than in writing. You use shorter, less complex sentences when speaking than when writing. Finally, intentional redundancies are built into the speaking processes that are not necessary in writing. This is because in writing you can always page back a page or two and figure out where you are, but you cannot do that with the spoken word. Once it is gone, it is gone (TIVO is altogether a different matter, of course). Aside from these differences, much of what you have learned about communication through your writing courses can be applied here to public speaking.

In both oral and written communication, considering the audience is critical. Regarding topic selection, it is important to know as much about your audience as possible – their knowledge base, their attitudes, beliefs and values, their demographics. The best speech given to the wrong audience is no longer the best speech. You inherently know this and adjust your oral communication daily when you speak differently to your peers than your grandparents. So, while you can chose a topic because you like it or know a lot about it – and that is a good starting place, do ask yourself why this particular audience should be informed about, persuaded of, or entertained by this topic. Once you have a topic in mind, you can move into preparing the introduction for your speech.

The introduction to your speech must accomplish four things. It can do more, but must at least do these four things to be successful. First, it must maintain your audience's attention in a favorable manner. Note I did not say "get your audience's attention" – you already have it – you are standing in front of them – they are looking at you. Now, keep it in a favorable way – this is your first chance to make a good impression – WOW them (this is called the primacy effect). Beebe and Beebe suggest many different ways to start your speech. You can open up your speech with illustrations, anecdotes, startling facts or statistics, quotations, humor, questions, references to historical or recent events, personal references, or references to the occasion or preceding speeches. Chose one of these methods and run with it. Please note that "Hi, my name is _____ and I wanna talk about…" is not listed as an effective opener. Avoid it.

The next three things can happen in any order – play around with them, just be sure that they are there. You need to establish audience relevancy – just a sentence or two that explicitly gives the audience a reason to listen to you for the next few minutes –assume they have the brain power of a bowl of oatmeal, and you can always be pleasantly surprised. Spell it out for them – something like, "You should be interested in this because …" is not too blatant – better that they know to pay attention now than for them to figure it out at the end of your speech, when it really is too late.

Another element of the introduction is to reveal the central idea of your speech. This statement is your thesis--the one, declarative, grammatically correct English sentence that sums up your whole speech. If you were to walk into class, and your instructor had just been informed of a campus-wide evacuation, but you had 15 seconds to deliver your speech, what is the one thing you would say? That is your central idea. It is the destination for your speech, where you want your audience to be at the end of your time with them.

The last task the introduction has to do is to preview the main ideas you will develop – the subdivisions of your speech. Just give the main points tag lines, little subtitles, and share those. If your speech's central idea is the destination, the preview of your main ideas is the road map for how you are going to get there.

So, this whole introduction can boil down to about four to six sentences, and usually should not take too long – 30 seconds to a minute in most cases. From the introduction you move to the body of your speech.

The body of your speech is divided into your main ideas, each of which moves you closer to the central idea of your presentation. This is where the bulk of your speech, the muscle that clings to the skeleton you presented in the introduction, is delivered. Here is where you make the case you are trying to present, whether that is informative, persuasive, or merely entertaining. You must have at least 2 main ideas (otherwise "main ideas" would not be plural) and should aim for 5 or less – your audience just will not remember more. Be sure to offer transitions between the main ideas – just a sentence or two that sum up where you just were and preview where you are going in the next main idea.

The order for your main ideas may come to you in a number of organizational patterns. They may just be areas that just seem to fit together, topically. The speech may be organized chronologically – step by step or by time periods. It may be organized spatially – by stories of a building, or what you would see as you looked left to right. The speech pattern may be cause and effect, or effects then causes. You can also organize you speech in a problem/solution format. As long as the order makes sense to you, and you can make it make sense to your audience, it is probably OK. Try to keep these main ideas approximately the same length, but do not obsess about it.

The body of your speech is where you cite the majority of the resources you used to research your speech. These citations of sources serve a number of purposes. It gets a bunch of experts up there with you, establishing your own credibility. It gives you something to talk about. It shows you are prepared for the speech. It probably fulfills part of the requirements for your assignment. It prevents accusations of plagiarism. So, this source citation process is important. Just as you verbally, out loud, to your audience, stated the central idea for your speech, you also need to share with the audience the sources you used. You should integrate these sources close to the relevant facts, not all at the beginning or all at the end of your speech. Just think of it as parenthetical notation out loud. The first page of this discussion shows parenthetical notation, (right under *The five cannons of rhetoric*) where I wanted to give credit where credit was due to Susan and Steven Beebe. You do the same thing in your speech. You need to give the audience enough information that we could find those facts for ourselves – either because your speech was great and we want to learn more, or because we want to verify the accuracy of something we doubt. To do this, tell us who wrote it and where you got it. Examples of this include: the author's name and book title; the magazine name and edition – title or author if available; the newspaper name and date; the sponsoring organization for a website and the day you accessed the information. Please note on the last example that we want the day you got the information – that way if we go and check and the information we see is different, we know if it was updated after you went there. Again, you have to tell your audience these source citations because they will never read your Reference page or see your Bibliography – all they have is what you tell them. This is a major difference between oral and written style.

As you finish preparing the body, the conclusion is in sight – there is the light at the end of your tunnel. Conclusions need to do three things. You restate the central idea- your one, last, best hope for the audience to get it. You restate the main ideas – just the tag line/titles again. And, just as you opened the speech up with a WOW statement, you want to WOW them at the end. Just as primacy effect holds that the first thing you say is really important, the recency effect maintains that the most recent thing, the last thing an audience hears from you, is vital as well. We've all had that uncomfortable feeling of not knowing whether or not to clap at what seems like the end of a presentation, but we are just not sure. Don't make your audience uncomfortable like that. Wrap it all up like a gift with a bow on top for them. The options for opening up your speech work for closing it as well. Ideally, if you started with a story, come back to the story; if you started with a statistic, end with a statistic; start and end with quotation – this process creates the impact you want.

Delivery styles

Each of the four main delivery styles has its benefits. Each also has its drawbacks. The four styles are manuscript, memorized, impromptu and extemporaneous. In this class we are encouraging you to develop your extemporaneous style.

Manuscript reading is writing out a speech and reading it to your audience. This allows for extensive preparation and exact word choices, but also risks greatly detracting from audience interaction and conversational delivery style. Most likely, until you are leader of the free world, nuclear Armageddon will not ride on your exact word choice, so it is probably preferable to have good interaction with your audience. Because of this, manuscript delivery is not often held up as a good option by most public speaking instructors. After all, your class is not one in Public Reading, so you will most likely be told not to deliver using this method.

Memorized delivery is when you write out the speech, then memorize it. This delivery style allows you to be free from notes, but still be prepared in advance. The problem with this style is fairly self-evident; you have no notes as a safety net. Now, this may sound like a good choice to those of you who were counting on manuscript delivery and are now panicking because you will not be able to just read a paper from another class to your Communication class. If you had seen how many times the *Word Fairy* refuses to come to students who have lost their place, however, you would no longer think it such a good idea. For those of you who are still tempted, remember the discussion above about the differences in oral and written communication style? When you write a speech and deliver it orally, it is the written style delivered orally, which just invariably doesn't sound right. Please trust me, it is not a good choice unless you have no other option.

Impromptu delivery is what many students try to pull off when they walk into class and go, "Oh, is that speech due *today*?" Often called winging it, speaking from the cuff, or pulling off a miracle (or other phrases I'm sure you can fill in), the main benefit to this style is immediacy with your audience, but the main drawback is that the speech is obviously not prepared in advance, and usually has no outside resource citations to flesh it out. It is good to work on your impromptu delivery skills, but not when large percentages of your grade ride on that presentation. There will be times when, in committees at work or in civic or volunteer organizations that you belong to, you will be put on the spot and asked to "Just say a few words for us." There is no need to panic in these situations. Just walk slowly to the front and think through your position – a simple central idea, and chose two or maybe three main ideas, and stay organized. It is amazing how much the simple act of organizing can improve an impromptu presentation. I still strongly recommend against this delivery style for your class presentations, unless your teacher has assigned this delivery style on purpose to work on these skills.

Extemporaneous delivery is the most commonly called for method of delivery in communication classrooms. This style is prepared in advance, but not completely written out, so it combines the benefits of early preparation with the immediacy of audience involvement. You use notes, preferably on note cards or legal pads, but not to read from them, just to use as delivery cues. Usually a good guideline is to use one notecard for the introduction, one notecard per main idea, and one notecard for the conclusion. Always write out your opener and closer as safety nets; write out your central idea as you have worked hard on the exact word choices, and you want to make that impact. Use tag lines for your main ideas, and include any statistics or quotations as well as the sources you are citing. Make a note to yourself to remember transitions. You can include instructions to yourself like, "Slow down here", "Pause here," "Make eye contact here", but be sure to put these in the margin or better yet, in a different color so you do not accidentally read out loud – "Check your fly." Be sure you have your initials on at least one of the cards, and number them. This is so when, not if, but when, you drop them, you can get them back in the correct order, quickly. It is likely that this is the style of delivery you will be instructed to use for your in class presentations.

Nervousness

First of all, please understand that nervousness/stage fright/ shyness/ communication apprehension is natural, and excessively normal. Most people have some degree of nervousness in some communication scenario. In a survey designed to identify the public's biggest fears, public speaking ranked #1, with a whopping 41 percent of the vote. Please recognize that the fear of death, death itself, ranked #6 in this survey. Fear of public speaking is very primal and inherent to the human condition. Were you any communal animal and the rest of the herd were all looking at you, it would be likely that you were going to be dinner. This is when the fight or flight reflex kicks in. When your heart is racing that means Adrenaline is rushing through your body, making logical thought nearly impossible. Neither fighting your audience nor fleeing them is a good informative, persuasive or entertaining strategy, so since those options are out, how do you manage the butterflies? Please note that I did not ask how you should get rid of them, as this is likely an unattainable goal, and one which I would not advocate if I thought you could do it. Yet, those exact same butterflies' wings give you vibrant energy and keep you on your toes during your speech. A lot of athletes are willing to take quite a physical pounding to get that same adrenaline rush – just think, you can have it without risk of permanent physical injury.

So, how do you manage your apprehension? Understanding and identifying it is the first step, recognizing that those around you are in the same boat should help quite a bit. Realize that you feel more nervous than you look, and have realistic expectations – the end of the world will not likely come about because you fumble over a word or two. Come up with the worst case scenarios, and debunk those you can. You are likely to discover that the worst case scenario is that you will be embarrassed, and maybe get a lower grade than you desired. Have those things ever happened to you before? Did you live through them? Of course, you did. You will this time, too. Hopefully your classroom has become a comfortable and safe environment, so feel free to take risks and learn from what goes well as well as from your mistakes. Public speaking is all over out there, so you may as well be good at it.

Take baby steps. In this or another class, ask a question. If that goes OK, answer a question. These are low risk public speaking endeavors. Go volunteer to read to a group of small children (NOT TEENAGERS) – you are an adult, and the fact that you are willing to spend time with them makes you infinitely awesome in their eyes – they are a great audience. Volunteer to read in your civic or religious organizations – you know those audiences, and they are likely to be supportive of your endeavors to better yourself. Join a group such as Toastmasters International who recognize the importance of public speaking, so give their members ample opportunities to practice.

Be prepared for your speech so you can be confident in your knowledge. Be sure you know your audience so that you know you have prepared correctly. Practice in a realistic environment enough to know your stuff, but not so much as to be stale. Have beady little eyes staring at you when you practice, friends or family preferably, but stuffed animals or a mirror work in a pinch. Visualize your success by taking a few moments before your speech to run through it – a positive attitude is not only helpful in the sports arena but here as well. Remember that if the topic was really so important that you wanted to give a speech on it to this audience, the topic is important enough that you should not be selfish about it. Thinking about yourself when you are up there, instead of what your audience needs, is really pretty selfish. You are better than that, and the topic is more important than that. Many of these hints are discussed in more detail in Beebe and Beebe (2006). Your instructor will also be willing to discuss hints with you, and please believe me that we have probably already taught people as nervous, if not more nervous, than you are. And, they all survived. You will too.

If this part of the class is exciting to you, consider joining our Nationally ranked speech and debate teams. If you have any Public Speaking questions, talk to your instructor. We teach this stuff for a bunch of reasons, but all include the fact that we like to talk, especially about communication. If you still have questions, come see me during office hours or make an appointment. I hope you have a memorable semester.

Reference

Beebe, S. A. & Beebe, S. J. (2006). *Public speaking: An audience centered approach. 6th ed.* Boston, MA: Allyn & Bacon.

A Guide to Interpersonal Communication: Student Handbook

Assignments

intro: trying on clasus /

body:
bathroom - prom

1
-
5

video clips

Presentation, Wed, 11th

(Team 1 or group A)

p. 84 with

typed assignment

Dyadic Evaluation Exercise

With your group, chose an artifact to base this assignment upon. Good options include a movie or television show or series. INDIVIDUALLY and INDEPENDENTLY type the answers to the following ten questions (this will be turned in – number the answers 1-10, do not make an essay out of the answers), then get the group together to discuss your answers.

conl.

• group picks

5 of 10

?'s

• visual handout
required

Your group will have 15 minutes of class time to present the 5 best answers as agreed upon by the group. You may use up to three video clips, but the combined length of those clips should not exceed 5 minutes. Each dyadic evaluation oral report should include: 1) no more than three clips from the same artifact(s); 2) a clear and knowledgeable presentation of at least three key communication concepts; 3) integration of visual aids and technologies; 4) strong organizational structure -- introduction, body and conclusion; and 5) overall effectiveness in terms of delivery and involvement of all speakers.

for presentation

1. Apply the elements of the linear model of communication to any conversation from your artifact. 0:27:00   w/ daughters . 41:00

⭐ 2. Discuss how one of the 8 principles of communication is demonstrated in your artifact. *principle 8*   p263   → mom was shougl

⭐ 3. Apply the Johari window to one of the characters in your artifact.

? 4. Identify each of the four types of cognitive schemata from your artifact. p. 75

5. Discuss the four dimensions of attributions in relationship to your artifact.

6. Tell us when language was arbitrary, ambiguous or abstract in your artifact.

7. Discuss how one of the principles of verbal communication was demonstrated in your artifact.

Comm.

8. Discuss how one of the principles of nonverbal communication was demonstrated in your artifact. Movie Clips p 135   1:11:30

hr 1:16:00

9. Identify what was to you the most noticeable nonverbal communication from your artifact and identify which type of nonverbal communication it was. 3 scene when his bored

10. Apply the six steps of the listening process to any conversation from your artifact.

scene after convo , dad & daughter at restaurant

Be sure to attach the evaluation sheet from the back of your student handbook to the written evaluation, and have the top part of the evaluation sheet completed for the oral report.

his personality

prototype -

stereotype - ladies man

personal construct — assertive, cocky , self absorbed

script - way he talks w/ women

visual
Handout — text from movie. (#10)

group → 45 pts
50 pts

Small Group Communication—Problem Solving Exercise

Adapted from Dewey's (1910) *How We Think*

Purpose/Objective:
*To gain problem solving and critical thinking skills through communicating in small groups.

Instructions: Your instructor will divide the class into 4 groups. Each group will be given a problem to solve. For this class exercise the necessary information will be provided.
Time Period One: Group A will observe Group C & Group B will observe Group D
Time Period Two: Group C will observe Group B & Group D observes A

The observing group will fill out the small group evaluation forms and discuss afterwards as a group how that group did in solving the problem.

Then the process will be reversed with the first participating groups observing the groups that were observing. The list below provides more detail about appropriate questions for each step. All of them do not have to be addressed. The list below is only to help you in the process, so one should study it before the event.

Evaluation: The emphasis is on following the procedure and using one's communication skills.

A: Observing Groups: As a group you have three observing forms to fill out and one summary form to share with the group you observed. You will want to have at least two people filling out each form as we know from observation that people do not interpret the same behavior the same way.
    The forms are:
> A) *Participation*
> B) *Problem Solving Sequence*
> C) *Leadership Tasks*
    Then you meet and decide how to evaluate the group on the *Group Evaluation Form*

B: Participating Groups: Read over the task first, marking appropriate information that you think you will be using. Then discuss the problem. Make sure that you are following the problem solving sequence. It will seem awkward at first, but it provides you with a systematic way of working through the problem. Provided below is more detail on each step. You will want this chart in front of you. After the observing group has evaluated you, then they will provide you with their summary evaluations and the supporting materials. Each person will fill out their own form on *Reflecting about our Group Activity*. Then you can compare your own evaluation with what is provided to you. You may use this form

Using Dewey's reflective thinking process consists of 6 steps.

1) Identify and define the problem

        Consider the following questions when attempting to identify and define a problem for group/team deliberations:
> a) What is the specific problem the group is concerned about?
> b) Is the question the group is trying to answer clear?
> c) What terms, concepts, or ideas need to be defined?
> d) Who is harmed by the problem?
> e) When to the harmful effects of the problem occur?

g. when he gets the box (facial expression hand gestures)

2) Analyze the problem

During the analysis of the phase of group/team problem solving, members need to research and investigate the problem. In analyzing the problem, a group/team may wish to consider the following questions:

a)   What is the history of the problem?
b)   How serious is the problem?
c)   What are the causes of the problem?
d)   What are the effects of the problem?
e)   What are the symptoms of the problem?
f)   What methods does the group/team already have for dealing with the problem?
g)   What are the limitations of those methods?
h)   How much freedom does the group/team have in gathering information and attempting to solve the problem?
i)   What are the obstacles that keep the group/team from achieving the goal?
j)   Can the problem be divided into sub problems for definition and analysis?

3) Develop criteria

Another phase in the analysis step of the reflective-thinking process is to formulate criteria for an acceptable solution. Criteria are the standards or goals for acceptable solutions. In listing criteria for a solution, you may wish to consider the following questions:

a)   What philosophy should the group/team adopt with respect to solving the problem?
b)   What are the minimum requirements of an acceptable solution?
c)   Which criteria are the most important?
d)   How should the group use the criteria to evaluate the suggested solutions?

Sample criteria for a solution may include the following:
1.   The solution should be inexpensive.
2.   The solution should be implemented as soon as possible.
3.   The solution should be agreed on by all of the team members.

4) Suggest possible solutions

After a group/team has analyzed a problem and selected criteria for a solution, it should begin to list possible solutions in tentative, hypothetical terms. Many teams suggest a variety of possible solutions without evaluating them.

5) Select the best solution(s)

After a team has compiled a list of possible solutions to a problem, it should be ready to choose the best solution according to the criteria listed. The following questions may be helpful in analyzing the proposed solutions:

a)   What would be the long-term effects and short-term effects of this solution if it were adopted?
b)   Would the solution really solve the problem?
c)   Are there any disadvantages to the solution? Do the disadvantages outweigh the advantages?
d)   Does the solution conform to the criteria formulated by the group?
e)   Should the group modify the criteria?

6) Test and implement the solution

Team members should be confident that the proposed solution is valid. In essence, the team should be confident that the solution will solve the problem. The team must then determine specifically how the solution can be put into effect. The following questions may be considered:

    a) How can the team get public approval and support for its proposed solution?

    b) What specific steps are necessary to implement the solution?

    c) How can the team evaluate the success of its problem-solving efforts?

In trying to apply reflective thinking to group/team problem solving consider the following:

1. Clearly identify the problem you are trying to solve.
2. Phrase the problem as a question to help guide group/team discussion.
3. Don't start suggesting solutions until you have analyzed the problem.
4. In the definition and analysis steps of reflective thinking, don't confuse the causes of the problem with its symptoms.
5. Constantly evaluate your team's problem-solving method.

Communication Symposium

Your group gets to lead class for 20 minutes about one of the concepts from your assigned chapter. The Symposium presentation is worth 100 points (shared by all members of your team); the peer and self evaluations of this project are worth 50 points; and the handout your group produces is worth 25 points.
Brief Overview:

Purpose: To provide students with an opportunity to work with other group members in designing and implementing a small group learning exercise. Students will be expected to facilitate/lead class in the activity. The assignment is designed to teach principles of small group processes.

Schedule:
Symposium Day 1 - Chapter 7   (team 1)
Symposium Day 2 - Chapter 8   (team 2)
Symposium Day 3 - Chapter 9   (team 3)
Symposium Day 4 - Chapter 10 (team 4)

Requirements:
1. Each group member must be equally involved in the assignment. If a group member does not participate in the planning process, the group may decide if he/she will take part in the exercise provided the following guidelines have been considered:
    a. Groups need to give a failing member advance notice that s/he is not meeting the group's expectations. Treat this as a professional encounter.
    b. The "problem group member" must be told what s/he must do to remain in the group and be given a chance to correct the behavior.
    c. Groups are discouraged from dismissing members at the last minute prior to their group presentation. It is your responsibility to handle problems early on in the process.
2. Because the focus is on active learning, the group should facilitate class participation as much as feasible; remember this is not a formal presentation to the class, but good presentation skills do count!
3. Provide a one-two page handout for every class member. This should include both an overview of the basic concept discussed and a reference list of resource material. Provide at least 4 references besides your textbook. Only 2 may be websites! One may be a movie, book or TV. show that highlights the concepts or principles discussed. Quality counts.
Here's your outline:

A) Climate setting/Ice breaker
B) Goal clarifying
C) Learning Experience
D) Processing
E) Generalizing and Applying
F) Closing

Group Information Sheet

Concept:_____ Date of Presentation:_____

Group Members and Contact Information:

Name   Phone   E-mail
_____

_____

_____

_____

_____

Meeting Times and Places:

_____

_____

_____

Possible Resources:

_____

_____

_____

_____

Conflict Reflection Essay Assignment

You have your choice of two versions of this assignment. Both involve a five-seven page essay.

Option 1) Chose an interpersonal (dyadic) conflict from your own life. Provide a brief (1-2 page) description of the background and content of this conflict. Discuss three principles of communication related to this conflict (1-2 pages). Apply those three principles to the scenario you have described (1-2 pages). Describe how this conflict could have gone differently if the conflict lessons learned from this text had been followed (1-2 pages).

Option 2) Chose an interpersonal (dyadic) conflict from a TV show or film. Provide a brief (1-2 page) description of the background and content of this conflict. Discuss three principles of communication related to this conflict (1-2 pages). Apply those three principles to the scenario you have described (1-2 pages). Describe how this conflict could have gone differently if the conflict lessons learned from this text had been followed (1-2 pages).

Good organization, grammar and formatting count. Your essay should have a coversheet and a reference page, even if the only reference used is your textbook. Use APA 5th edition for these formatting issues, and remember, the Writing Lab allows you ten appointments per semester, and your tuition dollars pay for these whether you use them or not. Be sure to attach the evaluation sheet from the back of your student handbook.

A Guide to Interpersonal Communication: Student Handbook

Optional Classroom Activities

Activity # 1
Community Builder Information Gathering Interview
Adapted from Dr. Sheryl Friedley, George Mason University

1. Select someone who will enable you to learn more about a club, organization, or co-curricular activity either at George Mason University (e.g., Learning in Retirement Institute, Pan Hellenic Association), in Fairfax County (e.g., Fairfax County Department of Community and Recreation Services, Generations Together, Generations United, Meals on Wheels, Humane Society, Wolftrap Associates), or on the national/international level (e.g., National Cancer Institute, Race for the Cure, Greenpeace, Audubon Society, Amnesty International, Peace Corps, Habitat for Humanity, Smithsonian Associates, National Museum for Women in the Arts, Kennedy Center for the Arts). Here's a helpful Internet site to get you started by punching in your zip code: www.volunteermatch.org

2. **OFFLIMITS: Close, personal friends or family members, sororities & fraternities**

3. Contact this individual; introduce yourself and your purpose. Arrange a 15-20 minute interview about the club, organization, or co-curricular activity you've selected. Ideally, you will do some homework about the organization and will be able to provide an interesting purpose for the interview beyond it being a class assignment. **Note: be sure to explain that you will need to audiotape the interview for your class and, at the time of the interview, *be sure that permission to do so is audible on tape*. (Automatic 10 pt. grade deduction without it) Videotaping is acceptable and same rules apply.**

4. Once you have arranged the interview, develop an interview guide that includes the following: 1) a written opener, 2) a written set of questions (10-15 questions) grouped under three or four topic areas – allow enough space after each question to write some brief notes on the interviewee's response, and 3) a written close. Be sure to use a minimum of 6 of the 7 types of questions, such as hypothetical or probing, which are discussed in your textbook. **TIP:** A good interview will show organization and focus. A laundry list of seemingly random questions is not an interview.

5. Prior to the interview, **which must be conducted in person**, check your equipment to make sure recorder, batteries, and tape are in good working order. At the interview, recheck and check also for ambient noise and distractions. Recording equipment is available through Audio Visual Services: 993-2206

6. On **the designated due date**, you will hand in the following information:
   a. a cover sheet that indicates who you interviewed, when you interviewed that individual, and where you interviewed that individual;
   b. the complete interview guide, including the written opener and closing, as well as the questions asked and any handwritten notes taken during the interview;
   c. the tape of your interview (cassette or mini-cassette is acceptable) with your name written clearly on it;
   d. a brief 1½ - 2 page paper that answers the following *four* questions:
      i. Why did you choose to interview someone from this club, organization, or activity?
      ii. What question and response do you feel provided you with the most valuable piece of information in this interview? Why?
      iii. If you could conduct the interview again, what might be something you would ask or do differently? Why?
      iv. What would you consider to be your greatest strength in conducting this interview? Why?

Activity # 1-B
Community-Builder Interview ~ Oral Report

Overview: This is a formal presentation of your interview results. You will need to briefly summarize why you chose to interview the person you did and what you learned about the organization during the interview. You may discuss the answers you gave to the questions addressed in the write up of your interview.

Requirements:
•Length: 3-4 minutes
  o   **(Note: timing of presentation is critical, so practice!)**
•You must have a definite introduction and conclusion
•Note cards only! You **must not** read your paper (or your note cards ~ so practice!)

Suggested:
Dress appropriately/professionally

Tips:
•Review public speaking basics in your text
•Practice, practice.
•Choose only the most interesting points to present
  o   Four minutes is not a long time
  o   Show enthusiasm for what you've learned
  o   Pretend you're trying to get your classmates to join or volunteer with this organization.
•Wait until you are at the front of the room or at the lectern before beginning to talk
•Talk a deep breath before you begin
•Make eye contact with our heads ~ sweep the room slowly, with pauses
•Watch the 'ums' and other annoying "fillers"
•Use transitions, signposts, and other strategies to keep your listeners oriented
•**SPEAK UP!!!!!!!!!**

Final note: There is a penalty for being over or under time, so practice!

Community-Builder Interview ~ Oral Report
Interview Project Presentation Format

INTRODUCTION

Attention Getter

√ Tell a story, read a quote, show a clip, ask a questions, etc.

Team member introductions

Thesis statement

Preview Points

Provide background information

√ Provide overview: purpose of interview & characters involved
√ Describe the climate of the interview

Transition...

BODY

Main Points

√ Discuss each point
√ Provide support with definitions, cites from text or video clips
√ Use transitions between each point

Transition...

CONCLUSION

Summarize thesis statement

Highlight major points discussed

Provide a "lasting impressions" closer

Activity #2
Alternate Format: Interview Critique/Panel Presentation
Adapted from Instructor Maria Chilcote

PURPOSE/ OBJECTIVE:
To provide an opportunity to apply interpersonal communication concepts learned in class through observing an interview, recording data and analyzing observations. In addition, you will have the opportunity to continue to enhance and hone your small group communication skills by engaging in another group presentation experience.

OVERVIEW:
This project has both an individual and a group component, *each* worth 100 points. Own their own, students will watch a pre-taped interview, record their observations and submit a paper answering prescribed questions on the interview. Afterwards, as a group, the students will discuss their observations and findings and then collaboratively deliver an informative presentation on their interview to the class.

REQUIREMENTS AND PROCEDURES:

Individual Interview Critique

1. Each group MUST watch the pre-recorded video that was assigned by the instructor. You may watch the video alone, with another group member or as an entire group.
2. While watching the interview, make notes on the Interview Critique form.
3. Once you have watched the video, type the answers to the questions listed on the Interview Critique form on a separate piece of paper. This paper must be typed in 12 pt. font, double-spaced, and contain both the question and the answer.
4. You will submit your paper, with the original Interview Critique Sheet (and any notes) attached, to the instructor in class on the designated due date. You will also use this paper as a point of reference for discussion with your group members in preparation for your presentation.

NOTE: This paper must cite SPECIFIC examples from the interview as well as concepts and principles from the text. For example, when writing about the climate of the interview – include both verbal and non-verbal communication aspects.

Group Presentation

1. Meet with all group members to prepare and practice your panel presentation. Use the Presentation Format as a guide. As with all group presentations, every member must have equal "air time."
2. Each panel presentation must have the following elements:

   √ **15 minutes in length**
   √ **Two video clips** from your interview to illustrate a point such as:
   - an example of a funnel sequence of questions

43

- a place where more probing was necessary
- an example where the interview*ER* was clearly prepared OR unprepared.

√ One other ***audio/visual component*** to use to illustrate a point e.g. handout, chart, poster, PowerPoint slide, overhead slide, etc.

3. **Address the following areas in your presentation:**

√ Give a brief ***overview*** of the interview including characters and purpose

√ What was the overall ***climate*** of the interview? Cite an example of either verbal or nonverbal communication that led to your perception.

√ How ***prepared*** was the interview*ER*? Cite specific examples of how you reached this conclusion.

√ Who had the ***balance of power*** during the interview? Provide concrete examples to back up your claim.

√ Give an example of ***person-centered communication*** on the part of the Interview*ER*. If none is present, provide an example of where s/he could have done a better job on this.

√ What were the predominant type (s) of ***question(s)*** used? Provide examples.

√ What was your ***favorite part*** of the interview? Why?

√ What special ***techniques*** did you observe that you could possibly use when in an interview situation (both from the interviewer and interviewee)

√ What ***behaviors***, if any, did you observe that you DO NOT want to portray in an interview? (either as an interviewer or interviewee)

√ What was your overall ***perception*** of the Interview*ER*? What behaviors led you to this?

√ Finally, switch hats and *briefly* critique the performance of the interviewee (just two or three observations)

Here is a checklist to remind you WHAT to bring with you to class on the day of your presentation:

PRESENTATION DAY CHECKLIST

_____Videotape of interview (cue clips BEFORE your presentation)

_____Any other visual aids

_____Team Evaluation sheet (1 per person)

_____Interview Critique form (1 per person)

Interview Critique

Grammar and spelling count! So proofread your typed responses before handing in. For some questions you'll want to tap into several concepts from your text and use examples from the interview to support your observations. You will be graded on the thoroughness, depth, and clarity of your responses. The point is for you to demonstrate your mastery of course material as well as understanding of fundamental principles of interviewing.

1. On a scale of 1-10, how **PREPARED** was the InterviewER to conduct this interview? On what are you basing this evaluation?

2. Describe the **CLIMATE** of the interview. Give an example of communication, either verbal or non-verbal, that helped set the climate.

3. Did the InterviewER demonstrate **PERSON-CENTERED COMMUNICATION**? If so, provide an example.

4. Who had the **"BALANCE OF POWER"** during the interview? Give an example of what that looked like.

5. What types of **QUESTIONS** were used? Cite an example of four different types (Open, Closed, Hypothetical, Probing, Summary, Mirror, Leading)

6. What special **TECHNIQUES** did you observe that you could possibly use when in an interview situation (as interviewer and/or interviewee)

7. What **BEHAVIORS** did you observe that you DO NOT want to portray in an interview? (as interviewer and/or interviewee)

8. What was your overall **PERCEPTION** of the interviewer – what behaviors led you to this assumption?

Additional Notes and Comments:

Activity # 3
Reflection/Observation
Adapted from Dr. Annika Hylmö

Directions: You may be assigned a specific topic or be asked to choose from the options provided below. Each essay requires 2-3 pages of writing and use of 4-5 concepts from the textbook/class discussions. Any writing or ideas taken from your textbook or other sources must be properly cited in your essay AND in a list of references at the end of your essay.

Journal 1:

For this assignment, think about some of the people whom you have met since the beginning of this semester. How did you decide which people you would like to get to know better, and which you were not as interested in? What were your perceptions of these people prior to really getting to know them better? How were your perceptions changed? Be honest with yourself! What do you think their perceptions of you were and how do you think those perceptions have changed? As you look at your perceptions and the attitudes that you discover, are there any attitudes that you would like to change? If so, which ones? What can you do to start the change?

Journal 2:

Remember a time when you heard someone call someone else using a word that made you react. How did you react? Why? Did you say something? Why or why not? Has anyone ever called you by a word that you didn't like? What was it, and how did you react? Have you ever called someone by a word that you thought was fine, but he or she didn't? What happened?

Journal 3:

For this journal, you are to act nonverbally in ways that are in complete discord with "normal" nonverbal communication. In other words, you might be standing in line and refuse to move forward when the line moves. You might be walking backwards across campus. You might be crying when you were supposed to be laughing. Pay close attention to the reactions that others give you. How do they react? What nonverbal communication do they rely on to convey to you how they perceive your communication?

Journal 4:

Describe your experience in the group that you just participated in. Are you satisfied with the quality of communication? How did communication in your group affect your work? How did communication in your group affect the outcome of your presentation? What are the group's strengths and weaknesses? How might you improve the situation prior to your next project?

Journal 5:

Think of an organization to which you belong. Identify rituals and rites in that organization and explain what they mean. What do they mean to you? What does it mean to participate?

Journal 6:

For this journal, think about how you perceive yourself. Monitor your communication for a few days. How are you communicating with others? How do you organize your perceptions? What does your communication reveal about your cognitive ability? Is there anything that you find disturbing about your communication? Then check your observations with someone else. To what extent do you agree with their perceptions of yourself?

ACTIVITY # 4
Name Bingo
Adapted from Dr. Lisa Sparks and Dr. Melinda M. Villagran

Purpose/Objective:
*To get to know fellow class members.

Instructions: Use one of the sample Bingo forms to play. Walk around the room and find students who have the characteristics in the squares. Write the corresponding names in the squares until you get a straight line horizontally, vertically or diagonally. Continue the game until each class member has at least one straight line. (You may also create new cards by filling in the blank Bingo forms with other characteristics.)

Rules: No talking other than to ask people their names! Go up to someone and point to a square you think "fits." If he or she indicates that it does, write the person's name in the square. If the person indicates that the characteristic does NOT fit, you may try ONE more square before moving on to other people. In other words, one person's name cannot be used in more than one square on your card, and you only have two chances to get a person's name on your card.

Find someone who...

B	I	N	G	O
Has more than one IM account	In a Sorority or fraternity	Has been to Italy	Is a freshman	Went to Catholic school
Has taken comm class before	Can teach a yoga or pilates class	Had an odd pet	Lives in the dorms	Was in a band
Knows someone famous	Attended another University	Plays basketball	Likes to download mp3s	Has a girlfriend or boyfriend
Has more than two sisters or brothers	Has never lived outside the DC area	Is a communication major	Knows how to create a web page	Has lived overseas
Can't swim	Is an art major	Likes country music	Has fallen in love before	Wants to be a doctor

Find someone who...

B	I	N	G	O
Has bought something on e-Bay	Is in a sorority or fraternity	Is related to royalty	Is a freshman	Does not like pizza
Has taken speech class before	Collects stamps	Is from another state	Lives in the dorms	Has eaten at the Johnson Center
Knows someone famous	Plays golf	Can't swim	Speaks at least three languages	Has never driven a car
Is an only child	Has never lived outside the DC area	Is a communication major	Knows how to cook an omelet	Currently practices a martial art
Can do a "stupid human trick"	Has been in a movie	Is colorblind	Had a pet rat	Drives a Jeep

Find someone who…

B	I	N	G	O
Had waffles for breakfast this morning	Can do the two-step	Works full-time	Sleeps on a waterbed	Loves sushi
Loves public speaking	Eloped	Is from another state	Has seen the movie *Matrix* more than twice	Went camping last summer
Knows someone famous	Has seen the sun rise at least once this year	Likes the color purple	Prefers country music to rock	Subscribes to the Wall Street Journal
Has been to Russia	Moved here within the past 6 months	Is a communication major	Maintains a blog	Can stand on his or her hands
Sneezes in bright sunshine	Has broken an arm or leg	Has acted on stage	Went to high school in a country other than the U.S.	Is married

Find someone who...

B	I	N	G	O
Has bought something on e-Bay	Can name the capital of Brazil	Is related to royalty	Is a freshman	Has taken dances lessons
Loves to read historical novels	Is a Redskins fan	Is from another state	Has a food allergy	Has eaten at the Johnson Center
Had a pet rat	Can whistle "America the Beautiful"	Has ambition to be President of the U.S.	Reads garden magazines	Has never driven a car
Is an only child	Has never lived outside the DC area	Has worked or volunteered in a library	Knows how to cook an omelet	Can do a cartwheel
Wears contact lenses	Has not seen the movie Da Vinci Code	Likes country music	Knows someone famous	Drives a Jeep

ACTIVITY # 5
Practicing the Art of Paraphrase
Adapted from Dr. Christine Smith

Students tend to rely too much on quoting the words of others in their writing. This poor writing practice may interfere with higher learning, because mere repetition is the least effective aid to long-term recall and understanding. Furthermore, students have a better grasp of ideas and concepts that they can put into their own words.

Purpose/Objective:
*To help students develop skills in paraphrasing material written by someone else.

Instructions: Read the following sentences from Wood's (2001) book, and then put the ideas expressed into your own words. An example is provided. Notice that the actual page number is provided with the quoted material, and only the author's name and year are cited with the paraphrased material.

From the text: "Ethnocentrism is a perspective based on the assumption that one's culture and its norms are the only right ones" (Wood, 2001, pp. 67-68).

Paraphrased: When one assumes that one's own culture and norms are the only right ones, one is expressing an ethnocentric view (Wood, 2001).

Now it's your turn:

According to Wood (2001), "People vary in their perceptions of the link between disclosure and intimacy. For some people talk is a primary way to develop intimacy, whereas other people regard sharing experiences and being together as more conducive to closeness than talking intimately" (p. 61).

Your version:

"Covert conflict exists when people camouflage disagreement and express it indirectly" (Wood, 2001, p. 71).

Your version:

"There is no objectively correct punctuation because it depends on subjective perceptions" (Wood, 2001, p. 90).

Your version:

"Dealing with diversity is a gradual process that requires time, experience with a variety of people, and a genuine desire to be part of a society that includes a range of people and communication styles" (Wood, 2001, p. 161).

Your version:

"Geographic separation can be difficult for friends and romantic couples. Many of us will be involved in long-distance romantic relationships because they are increasingly common. Fully 70% of college students are or have been in long-distance romances (Rohlfing, 1995), and even more have been or are involved in long-distance friendships. The number of long-distance relationships is likely to increase in the years ahead" (Wood, 2001, p. 205).

Your version: (note: to cite both Rohlfing and Wood properly, see your Style Manual)

ACTIVITY # 6
Types of EVIDENCE
Adapted from Dr. Christine Smith

Purpose/Objectives: *To familiarize students with the types of evidence used in persuasive and informative communication.

Instructions: This activity may be done at home, in class, alone or in groups. Evidence may be collected from all types of media, but magazines are likely to be the most convenient.

Review the types of evidence discussed in your textbook. Find examples of each to share with the class. Be especially watchful for examples that you feel are inaccurate, untruthful, or misleading. What is the target audience?

Be prepared to discuss your examples in terms of their purposes and relative success.

Notes:

ACTIVITY # 7
The Ideal Visual Aid Would Be...
Adapted from Dr. Lisa Sparks and Dr. Melinda M. Villagran

Purpose/Objective:
*To help students begin to brainstorm visual aids which they might use in their own and/or team presentations.

Instructions: Divide into groups and decide what the **ideal** visual aid would be for the following presentations. Consider the various types of visual aids (videos, flow charts, bar charts, graphs, slides, photographs, etc.) and decide how you would present them in the context of each presentation.

1. An informative demonstration speech explaining how to listen effectively.

2. An informative presentation about the Johari Window.

3. A persuasive speech opposing Internet citations.

4. An informative speech about turning points.

5. A persuasive speech in favor of multicultural education in health care settings.

6. An informative demonstration speech explaining how to communicate with your family.

ACTIVITY #12
Bias-Free Language
Adapted from Dr. Lisa Sparks and Dr. Melinda M. Villagran

Purpose/Objective:
*To help students understand how to utilize bias-free language.
* To let students practice rephrasing words in order to communicate in a bias-free manner.

Instructions:
Class members should read the following passage. Identify biased language and choose bias-free replacements for those words. Replacement words should not change the overall meaning of the passage. Choose one student to write the biased words and their replacements on the board.

Read the following:

Tai is a Vietnamese fireman who was born in California. One day, he got a call for a fire at the house of a 24-year-old girl named Elizabeth. When Tai and his fire crew pulled up to the address they were given at the firehouse, they saw an old geezer sitting on the porch. "Where is the fire," asked Tai. The old man was deaf so he did not hear Tai's question. At that moment, Tai heard a girl yell, "Hey, the fire is over here!" He quickly drove his fire truck to the next street where he saw Elizabeth's burning house. Tai quickly turned on his fire hoses to fight the fire. He knew that he had to hurry and get the situation under control because he was the only man there (and men are always braver than women). Finally the fire was extinguished. All of mankind should be grateful for brave men like Tai.

ACTIVITY #10
Supporting Materials
Adapted from Dr. Lisa Sparks and Dr. Melinda M. Villagran

Purpose/Objective:
*To understand the importance of using evidence to support claims.
*To learn how to incorporate evidence into papers.

Instructions:
Students should choose a magazine article or advertisement that uses statistics to support a claim. Watch for the use of implied statistics without any numbers to back up the statistics (e.g., more doctors prefer drug A). Each student will have the opportunity to analyze the article and provide an explanation for the class:

(1) What type of statistics is used in the article?

(2) What claim are the statistics included to support?

(3) Does the article include information about the origin of the statistics (who did the research)?

(4) Does the article effectively use the statistics to make an argument? Why or why not?

ACTIVITY # 10
Listening
Adapted from Barra Kahn, George Mason University

Purpose/Objective: To enable students to experience both nonlistening and active, mindful listening. This exercise is for the entire class. Form two circles in the center of the room: an inner circle facing out, and an outer circle facing in. Each person should be facing another person in a dyad. The people in the inner circle need to think up a problem (they can choose either something real happening in their lives, or make one up) and take one minute to tell "the problem" to their dyad partner.

The dyad partner (the first listener) must listen as a <u>monopolizer</u> would (timed: one minute). Then everyone in the outer circle takes one step to the left, and has a new dyad partner. Now the people in the inner circle tell the *same story* to their new partner (one minute), who is a <u>pseudolistener</u> (one minute to respond); then everyone in the outer circle steps one person to the left. Now the people in the inner circle (with still new dyad partners) tells the same sad story to their new dyad partner (one minute) who is a <u>defensive listener</u> (one minute response); outer circle steps one person to the left; and finally the person in the center tells their story one last time to their fourth dyad partner who is a <u>committed listener</u>.

After the committed listener gets her turn, the outer circle steps one to the left, and the new dyad partners switch places so the people on the inside are now on the outside, and vice versa. They repeat the process with the new inner circle telling the story, and the outer circle responding as monopolizer, pseudolistener, defensive listener, and committed listener, only this time stepping one person to the right, so as not to repeat partners.

It doesn't matter which forms of nonlistening are used, but it is important that the last time the story is told, it is told to a committed listener, so the story teller can effectively feel the difference between not being heard, and then finally being heard.

Ask yourself:

Which type of listening do you think you do most?
What does it feel like to be really heard by a committed listener?

ACTIVITY # 11
Outlining
Adapted from Dr. Lisa Sparks and Dr. Melinda M. Villagran

Purpose:
*To help students understand the importance of clear, concise outlining.
*To show students how to look for proper coordination and subordination when preparing an outline.
*To teach students how to organize papers by extracting an outline from an academic journal article.

Instructions:
Students should get into small groups (4 or 5). Each group is responsible for bringing one academic journal article from the library. Students should identify the main purpose of the article; an introduction consisting of an attention-getter, establishment of ethos, and a preview/thematic statement; three main points with sub- and sub-sub points, and a conclusion summarizing the main theme, reviewing each major point, and a creative concluding thought. Each group should then briefly tell the class the steps taken in outlining their particular article.

. ACTIVITY #12:
Who Am I?
(And how did I get this way?)
Adapted from Dr. Christine Smith

Purpose/Objective: *To reveal that the many ways we see ourselves evolve over time via interaction; our self-concept is both personal and social.

Fill in the blanks. Work quickly without thinking too much. There are no wrong answers when describing one self.

I am _____ .

I am _____ .

I am _____ .

I am _____ .

I am _____ .

I am _____ .

I am _____ .

I am _____ .

I am _____ .

I am _____ .

What have you just revealed about yourself?

How many responses are role labels?

How many are personal descriptors?

How many are identity scripts?

Who told you that you were these things?

Who do we compare ourselves to on personal constructs such as friendliness, trustworthiness, compassion, intelligence? Are these bases for comparison realistic?

Are positive comparisons (e.g., I am smart) made on the basis of prototypes, such as "I'm pretty smart, like Einstein," or based on negative experiences closer to home? "Compared to cousin Jimmy, I'm a genius.")

What about negative experiences? "I'm so skinny!" Who are we comparing ourselves with and why? Compare me to a model... is that realistic? Compare me to myself when I was a teenager. Is THAT realistic?

ACTIVITY #13:
Semantic Reactions
Adapted from Dr. Christine Smith

SEMANTIC REACTIONS-<u>WHAT INFORMS MEANING????????</u>

<u>PURPOSE:</u> To examine your own semantic reactions to words, in order to clarify why "the meanings are in people, not words."

This exercise makes us take a look at what **<u>informs</u>** the meaning of words for us. The more we understand language, its nuance and specificity, the more clarity drives our communication.

<u>PROCEDURE:</u> Below is a list of words. Rank each word based on your immediate reaction. You need not know the meaning of a word in order to have a response. (You may, for example, respond to the sound or sight of the word.) This activity is to allow you to examine your semantic reactions, so be as aware and honest as possible.

Rating Scale: 1= Highly positive   3= Negative
                2= Positive   4= Highly Negative

____1. Patriotism	____34. Church
____2. Republican	____35. Religion
____3. Democrat	____36. Bedroom
____4. Lawyer	____37. Indian
____5. Doctor	____38. Football
____6. Policeman	____39. Theatre
____7. Dog	____40. Math
____8. Cat	____41. Housework
____9. Shakespeare	____42. Motorcycle
____10. Feminist	____43. Polyester
____11. Homosexual	____44. Military
____12. Menstruation	____45. Marriage
____13. Castrate	____46. Lesbian
____14. Death	____47. Science
____15. Sex	____48. Art
____16. Internet	____49. Sports
____17. Breast	____50. Cooking
____18. Family	____51. Gay
____19. Authority	____52. Spirit
____20. Oyster	____53. Den
____21. Gun	____54. Wedding
____22.computer	____55. Sanctuary
____23. Money	____56. Yard
____24. School	____57. Museum
____25. Hispanic	____58. Exercise
____26. Islam	____59. Vote
____27. Politician	____ 60. Congress
____28. Kitchen	
____29. Pregnant	
____30.television	
____31. Literature	
____32. Teacher	
____33. Jew	

1. Did your semantic reactions differ from others?
2. Which responses to words were the same? Different?
3. On what were your reactions based? Does this teach us something about the highly subjective aspects of language? What is the role of personal experience?
4. With respect to semantic reactions, what suggestions could you make to improve communication? What is semantic integrity? Authentic meaning?
5. How does this exercise enlighten us as to communication breakdowns?
6. Is it possible to know the meaning of a word out of context?
7. Think about your strongest reactions to the words. Upon what factors were they based (e.g., sex, race, religion, income, age)?

ACTIVITY #14
Communication Climate
Adapted from Barra Kahn, George Mason University

Supportive Climates

Descriptive communication
Provisional communication
Spontaneous communication
Problem Oriented communication
Empathic communication
Equality fostering communication

Defensive Climates

Evaluative communication
Certain communication
Strategic communication
Controlling communication
Neutral communication
Superiority communication

Working in groups, use one type of relationship (i.e., friendship, romantic partnership, spouse, parent, child, sibling, boss, etc.), and provide an example that illustrates each of the forms of communication above. Then discuss, as a class, how relational partners are likely to respond to these messages. Individually, think about how often you use supportive or defensive communication strategies in your important relationships. Talk about ways in which we might switch defensive behaviors into supportive behaviors.

ACTIVITY #15
Breaking Nonverbal Rules
Adapted from Brigitte Hinkle, George Mason University

Form student pairs. One student in each pair is designated as the rule-breaker and the other is the observer. The task of the rule-breaker is simply to enter some campus situation in which one or more rules of nonverbal communication would normally be operative and to break one or more rules. The task of the observer is to record mentally (or in writing, if possible) what happens as a result of the rule breaking. Note, for example, both verbal and nonverbal responses to the situation. Age and gender differences may also be observed. Feel free to compare responses in different contexts.

Caveats:
- Do not infringe on the rights and well being of others
- Do not violate the law
- Do not use cars or other motor vehicles as a means to violate the rules

Examples for rule breaking:

Enter an elevator and stare at the back of the elevator or stand very close to another person

Sit next to someone and invade that person's private space with your body or your belongings

When strangers are talking, enter their group discussion

When talking with someone, stand too close or too far away

When talking in an occupied area, talk louder so that others are disturbed by your conversation

Be creative!

ACTIVITY #16:
Generations
Adapted from Dr. Terri Wray

Intergenerational Communication Activity

Out of Class:

Select a family member who is either about 30 years older or 30 years younger than you are to interview. (If you don't have access to a family member you may select some other person who fits the age criteria. Retirement homes will have people willing to speak with you). Your purpose for this interview is to uncover cultural aspects of your family's, or another family's history that interest you (see the chapter on adapting to others).

Quickly plan your interview, by preparing at least 10 questions ahead of time (see the appendix on interviewing for interviewing guidelines.) Set up the interview: allow approximately 1-2 hours to complete the interview. Ask for permission to take quick notes during the interview and jot down answers.

In Class:

The instructor will place you into small groups according to the categories of interviewees (like 80-year-olds and above, etc). Your group will create an in-class presentation to teach us about this age culture.

ACTIVITY #17
Advice...Advice
Adapted from Dr. Terri Wray

Using "Advice Columns" to Stimulate Discussion

Purpose/Objective: *To stimulate discussion about how interpersonal problems and issues may be understood (and managed) via theoretically-based principles and concepts of communication. Also, to provide students with the opportunity to facilitate a discussion.

Good Source: "Tell Me About It: Advice for the Under-30 Crowd" by Carolyn Hax in *The Washington Post,* Style Section, on Fridays and Sundays. You may also check "Miss Manners," "Dear Abby," "Ann Landers," or alternatives such as Dr. Phil.

In "Tell Me About It" a young woman wrote that her sister was "driving [her] nuts" by phoning her several times each day, interrupting her work. The young woman said the calls were "unimportant" or could really wait until she got home from work. She asked her sister not to call her at work, but the sister continued to call her there, asking "if [she] was busy" yet ignored the "yes" answer, and continued to "just quickly tell" her something anyway. Her sister also calls her at home, interrupting dinner, etc., and asks "am [I] too easy on her?" This letter could be used to illuminate a variety of interpersonal concepts: (1) aggressive/assertive/deferential communication; (2) conflict, overt and covert (passive aggression); (3) confirming/disconfirming messages; (4) evaluative/descriptive language, and others.

Instructions: Select a letter that can be used to start a class or group discussion. Put it on an overhead transparency (or some other available medium). Put the columnist's response on a separate transparency, in case you want to withhold the response until the end of the discussion (with some letters, the point of discussion may actually be in the answer). Be prepared to facilitate discussion by indicating why you think the letter is a good example of _____, asking questions, and keeping class on topic.

ACTIVITY #18

Tic-Tac-Terms
Adapted from Dr. Lisa Sparks and Dr. Melinda M. Villagran

Purpose/Objective:
*To learn communication terms and their definitions

Instructions:
This game is much like tic-tac-toe, except it teaches communication-related terms. Students should bring nine pennies to class (or tear nine small pieces of paper to use for game pieces). Draw a tic-tac-toe board below (three rows and three columns). The instructor will call out all of the terms from the chapter and each student will select nine of them and write them in each space of the board below. The instructor will call out the definitions of all the terms without giving the actual word or term. Students will mark the words they have on their card by recognizing the definition when it is called out. When a student gets three terms in a row (horizontal, vertical, or diagonal lines), he or she wins that round. Halfway through the class period, students may select new terms to put on their card.

Activity #19
Communication Question Bingo: Instructor/Facilitator Instructions

Materials needed:

1. 25 fill-in-the-blank questions

2. 25 small pieces of paper numbered with 1 to 25

3. Stopwatch

4. Prizes, if desired (such as bags of candy or snacks; hokey toys related to communication, like toy phones; telephone of cans and string; used books: *The Intimate Enemy, Getting to Yes, The Road Less Traveled, You Just Don't Understand: Men and Women in Conversation, etc.*; Booby prize: picture of the instructor (Xeroxed)

Object of game:
To answer the questions correctly until a group has 5 answered questions in any vertical, horizontal, or diagonal order on its card, allowing the group to call "Bingo."

Before the game starts:
1. Have students sit together in their groups
2. Go over the materials and object of game
3. Have class decide how much time for each question -- 30 seconds to 90 seconds
4. Have class read Student Instructions. (~ 2 mins.)
5. Note: Students can use class notes, text, workbook, any materials provided

During the game:

1. Choose question number (random) from the "Bingo Bag"
2. Read the question that corresponds to that number.
3. Begin timing when finished reading.
4. Repeat the question twice during the time.
5. When time is up draw a new number and repeat Steps 2 through 4.
6. Teams can call Bingo whenever they believe they have a Bingo.

7. When Bingo is called: Group states the 5 Bingo question #s it has in a row and has answered. (Instructor reads each corresponding question and group gives the answer.)

8. Do not provide class with the correct answer for any incorrect responses (so they will continue to try to find the correct answer).

9. If incorrect answer: that group MAY NOT use the incorrect question number again in the same Bingo line, but it MAY use the question number in a different Bingo line (this prevents students from merely changing their answers (or guessing) and trying for the same "Bingo" again.

10. Keep track of Bingo group participants, Bingos called, and points on the Bingo Group lists.

11. *The game is OVER when* all 25 questions have been asked or all groups have earned a "true" Bingo (the game's end) explain incorrect answers, or unanswered questions, to the class.

Bingo: *Student Instructions*

1) Your group needs
   - bingo card and bingo chips
   - each member can use class readings, handouts, notes, etc. to find answers
   - recorders (to jot down Q & A) for questions and answers 1-25 (you will not receive a copy of the questions)

2) *Object of game:*
   - to place 5 chips in a vertical, horizontal or diagonal row
   - group calls "Bingo" when it has found the correct answer. (Groups may continue to search for answers to previously read questions while new questions are being worked on. "Bingo" may be called whenever a group believes they have a true bingo.)

3) *Instructor:*
   - selects random number from the bag
   - reads that numbered question once
   - starts timing
   - repeats the question once or twice more during the timed period
   - when time is up, if no Bingo has been called, draws a new number for the next question

4) *When Bingo is called:*
   - instructor selects the group she heard call "Bingo" first
   - the group reads its five numbers
   - instructor records the Bingo
   - instructor reads each question and tells the group which are true and which are not

5) *Incorrect answers:*
   - may NOT be used for that group in that same bingo line
   - but may be used for a different bingo line.

6) *Game ends when:*
   - all questions have been asked, or
   - all groups have earned a "true" Bingo.

Bingo numbers – These are the numbers that, when drawn, determine which question is read aloud. Separate them and put the squares into bag, hat, box, or basket

1	2	3	4	5
6	7	8	9	10
11	12	13	14	15
16	17	18	19	20
21	22	23	24	25

Bingo Card – Randomly number your own squares (1-25)

Leave room to write your answers

Bingo Card

BINGOS CALLED:

Group#	Question #s w/correct responses	Question #s w/incorrect responses

BINGOS CALLED:

Group#	Question #s w/correct responses	Question #s w/incorrect responses

BINGOS CALLED:

Group#	Question #s w/correct responses	Question #s w/incorrect responses

A Guide to Interpersonal Communication: Student Handbook

Grading and Evaluation Forms
(to turn in w/ assignments)

Small Group Participation Evaluation Form

Instructions: The goal of this observation is to record and classify the participation that each person is making. In group discussion on can try to have comments that can be classified as a) content comments, b) climate building comments, or c) leadership comments. Thus, each time a person you are observing is speaking you classify the comments. Sometimes a comment can cover two or more functions so mark all three areas.

As a group decide which persons you will be observing. Make sure that each person in the participating group has 2 or more observers. That means you will be observing most times only three people.

Person Being Observed	Content Comments	Climate Comments	Leadership Comments	Total # of Comments
Jared	✓✓✓✓ ✓✓✓✓	✓✓✓✓✓✓ ✓✓✓✓ ✓✓	✓✓✓✓✓	30
yellow shirt	✓✓✓✓ ✓✓✓✓✓ ✓	✓✓✓ ✓✓✓	✓✓✓✓✓ ✓✓	

Note: You may want to calculate the % of the types of comments the person observed made. For example, if the person made 12 comments [8 content; 2 climate, and 2 leadership] then you divide each type by the total. In the example it would mean the person had 67% content comments and about 17% of that person's comments were for climate and another 17% were about leadership.

Small Group Evaluation Form: Problem-Solving Discussion

Instructions: Have one or two people in the observing group focus on the problem solving discussion as to the steps that need to be taken. The task here is to answer the questions and make an evaluation of how effective the group was with each step of the sequence. A 5 point scale will be used to evaluate how well each step was completed. The observer needs to make notes on what was done so that the rationale for the judgment can be provided.

Step I: Define the Problem

Step II: Analyze the problem

Step III: Develop a Criteria

Step IV: Propose Solutions

Step V: Consider Each Solution

Step VI: Select a Solution

Evaluation:

1. Defines the Problem	1	2	3	4	5
2. Analyzes the Problem	1	2	3	4	5
3. Develops a Criteria	1	2	3	4	5
4. Proposes Solutions	1	2	3	4	5
5. Considers Each Solution	1	2	3	4	5
6. Selects a Solution	1	2	3	4	5

1= weak   5=done well

Small Group Evaluation Form: Leadership Tasks

Instructions: Have 1 or 2 people in the group evaluate the achievement of the leadership tasks. Rate on a 5 point scale how well the group achieved the tasks listed. The purpose of the feedback is to help the group do better the next time they are in a decision making group, so honesty is an important task here. Review the tasks in the reading before using this form. You need to fill out the form after the group is done.

The group did the following tasks during the session

The purpose was clarified	1	2	3	4	5
Balanced Participation was achieved	1	2	3	4	5
Kept group on task so that they finished on time	1	2	3	4	5
Internal Summaries were made so members knew where they were in the process	1	2	3	4	5
The decision was made with all members having input	1	2	3	4	5
The decision was summarized	1	2	3	4	5
All members had a chance to speak and share opinions	1	2	3	4	5

Observers Suggestions to the GROUP to improve on leadership tasks.

1.

2.

3.

4.

Evaluator: _____

Communication Symposium Evaluation Form: Peer & Self Evaluation

DO THESE PRIOR TO YOUR PRESENTATION (comments *must* be made on each person)

Your name:_____

Team member's name: <u>YOU</u>_____

<u>Always attended meetings</u>	10 9 8 7 6 5 4 3 2 1	Seldom or never attended meetings
<u>Available when needed</u>	10 9 8 7 6 5 4 3 2 1	Seldom available when needed
<u>High quality of work</u>	10 9 8 7 6 5 4 3 2 1	Low quality of work
<u>Dependable</u>	10 9 8 7 6 5 4 3 2 1	Undependable
<u>Facilitated goal achievement</u>	10 9 8 7 6 5 4 3 2 1	Hindered goal achievement
<u>Overall high evaluation</u>	10 9 8 7 6 5 4 3 2 1	Overall low evaluation

Comments:

Team member's name: _____

<u>Always attended meetings</u>	10 9 8 7 6 5 4 3 2 1	Seldom or never attended meetings
<u>Available when needed</u>	10 9 8 7 6 5 4 3 2 1	Seldom available when needed
<u>High quality of work</u>	10 9 8 7 6 5 4 3 2 1	Low quality of work
<u>Dependable</u>	10 9 8 7 6 5 4 3 2 1	Undependable
<u>Facilitated goal achievement</u>	10 9 8 7 6 5 4 3 2 1	Hindered goal achievement
<u>Overall high evaluation</u>	10 9 8 7 6 5 4 3 2 1	Overall low evaluation

Comments:

Team member's name: _____

<u>Always attended meetings</u>	10 9 8 7 6 5 4 3 2 1	Seldom or never attended meetings
<u>Available when needed</u>	10 9 8 7 6 5 4 3 2 1	Seldom available when needed
<u>High quality of work</u>	10 9 8 7 6 5 4 3 2 1	Low quality of work
<u>Dependable</u>	10 9 8 7 6 5 4 3 2 1	Undependable
<u>Facilitated goal achievement</u>	10 9 8 7 6 5 4 3 2 1	Hindered goal achievement
<u>Overall high evaluation</u>	10 9 8 7 6 5 4 3 2 1	Overall low evaluation

Comments:

Your name:

Team member's name: _____

Always attended meetings	10 9 8 7 6 5 4 3 2 1	Seldom or never attended meetings
Available when needed	10 9 8 7 6 5 4 3 2 1	Seldom available when needed
High quality of work	10 9 8 7 6 5 4 3 2 1	Low quality of work
Dependable	10 9 8 7 6 5 4 3 2 1	Undependable
Facilitated goal achievement	10 9 8 7 6 5 4 3 2 1	Hindered goal achievement
Overall high evaluation	10 9 8 7 6 5 4 3 2 1	Overall low evaluation

Comments:

Team member's name: _____

Always attended meetings	10 9 8 7 6 5 4 3 2 1	Seldom or never attended meetings
Available when needed	10 9 8 7 6 5 4 3 2 1	Seldom available when needed
High quality of work	10 9 8 7 6 5 4 3 2 1	Low quality of work
Dependable	10 9 8 7 6 5 4 3 2 1	Undependable
Facilitated goal achievement	10 9 8 7 6 5 4 3 2 1	Hindered goal achievement
Overall high evaluation	10 9 8 7 6 5 4 3 2 1	Overall low evaluation

Comments:

Team member's name: _____

Always attended meetings	10 9 8 7 6 5 4 3 2 1	Seldom or never attended meetings
Available when needed	10 9 8 7 6 5 4 3 2 1	Seldom available when needed
High quality of work	10 9 8 7 6 5 4 3 2 1	Low quality of work
Dependable	10 9 8 7 6 5 4 3 2 1	Undependable
Facilitated goal achievement	10 9 8 7 6 5 4 3 2 1	Hindered goal achievement
Overall high evaluation	10 9 8 7 6 5 4 3 2 1	Overall low evaluation

Comments:

Small Group Experiential Learning Assignment Evaluation Form

Names: _____   Concept_____

Each Experiential Learning workshop should include: 1) a one page synopsis of the major conceptual issues with list of sources; 2) a clear and knowledgeable demonstration of key concepts with integration of visual aids and technology; 3) group facilitated/encouraged class participation and discussion; 4) strong organizational structure -- choice of opener, exercise, and closure appropriate for the communication concepts; and 5) overall effectiveness in terms of delivery and involvement of all speakers.

Evaluation Category   Points/

1. Quality of handout (e.g., summary of major conceptual issues).   _____/20

2. Demonstration of key concepts (e.g., goals are clear, visual aids/technology)   _____/20

3. How well the workshop involved members of the class.   _____/20

4. Organizational structure   _____/20

5. Overall effectiveness (e.g., delivery involved all speakers)   _____/10

6. Peer evaluation   _____/10

Comments

Strong points

Weak points

_____

Emailed materials to instructor and commbc?   yes   no=0

e.g.: gbush1-101-001-grouplearning.doc *and* **gbush1-101-001-groupslides.ppt**

Time _____ **Penalty** _____

                                                        TOTAL____/100

82

Communication Symposium Team Presentation Evaluation Form

(one per team please, fill out top section **prior to** class)

Your team's members' names: Chapter:_____

_____   Concept : _____

_____

_____

_____

_____

_____

Each group project should include: 1) a one-two page synopsis of the major conceptual issues with a list of sources; 2) a clear and knowledgeable presentation of key concepts with integration of visual aids and technologies; 3) group facilitated/encouraged class participation and discussion; 4) strong organizational structure -- choice of opener, exercise, and closure appropriate for the communication concepts; and 5) overall effectiveness in terms of delivery and involvement of all speakers.

Evaluation category   Points

1. Organizational structure   ____/20

2. Delivery (includes division of labor within group)   ____/20

3. Demonstration of key concepts (e.g. goals are clear and well met) ____/20

4. Class Involvement   ____/10

5. Use of handout/visual aids/technology   ____/10

6. Overall effectiveness (e.g. delivery involved all speakers)   ____/ 20

7. Time _____/20 minutes   Penalty____

                                                     Total ____/100

Comments:

Outline   Strong Points:

Weak Points:

83

Dyadic Oral Report Evaluation Form

(one per team please, fill out top section **prior to** class)

Your group's members' names:

Artifact:_____

_____   Communication Concepts discussed:

_____   _____

_____   _____

_____   _____

_____

_____

Each dyadic evaluation oral report should include: 1) no more than three clips from the same artifact(s); 2) a clear and knowledgeable presentation of at least three key communication concepts; 3) integration of visual aids and technologies; 4) strong organizational structure -- introduction, body and conclusion; and 5) overall effectiveness in terms of delivery and involvement of all speakers.

Evaluation category	Points
1. Organizational structure	____/20
2. Delivery (includes division of labor within group)	____/20
3. Definitions and descriptions of key concepts	____/20
4. Choice of artifact and scene selection	____/10
5. Application to artifact	____/20
6. Use of visual aids/technology	____/15
7. Overall effectiveness (e.g. delivery involved all speakers)	____/20

8. Time _____/20 minutes   Penalty____

Total ____/125

Comments:

Outline   Strong Points:

Weak Points:

Information Gathering Interview Evaluation Form

Interviewer_____

Content and Structure:

Opening   _____/10

Body
Structured Approach, used transitions   _____/10
Primary Questions   _____/10
Secondary/Probing Questions   _____/10

Closing   _____/10

Interview Communication Skills:
Verbal   _____/10
Control & Pacing   _____/10

Written Materials:
Background Cover Sheet   _____/10
Completed Interview Guide   _____/10
Organizational Structure   _____/10

Permission to record interview audible on tape?   Yes _____   No   (-10 if not)

Additional Comments:

_____

Email attachment(s) to instructor /commbc   yes   no=0
                                                                        TOTAL _____/100

Reflection/Observation Essay Evaluation Form

Audience Analysis/Topic Choice
Subject is relevant to communication phenomena   _____/5

Paper Organization/Application
Organizational structure is solid   _____/5
Analysis is thorough   _____/5
Analysis is insightful   _____/5
Concepts chosen are applicable and appropriate   _____/5
Explanations/definitions of concepts are sufficient and properly credited   _____/5

Writing Style
APA style is used correctly throughout paper   _____/1
Paper uses active voice when possible   _____/1
Paper avoids gender specific pronouns   _____/1
Easily understandable & grammatically correct sentence structure is used   _____/1
Paper does not include slang or clichés   _____/1
Paper does not include misspelled words   _____/1
Paper does not include grammar mistakes   _____/1
Paper is written in appropriate language with no contractions   _____/1
Paragraphs begin with a thesis sentence   _____/1
Each paragraph includes several supporting sentences   _____/1

Requirements
Number of integrated concepts utilized is appropriate and correct (4-5)   _____/5
Paper excluding references fulfills length requirement for assignment (2-3)   _____/5

Total Score   _____/50

Email attachment to instructor and commbc   yes   no=0
Grade   _____

Midcourse feedback

Comm 101: Section # _____

	Too slow		Fine		Too Fast
How is the pace of the course for you?	1	2	3	4	5

	Too easy		Fine		Too Hard
How is the difficulty of the material?	1	2	3	4	5

	Not enough		Fine		Too Much
Is the amount of material right?	1	2	3	4	5

	No		Some		A lot
Do the lectures help you understand the material?	1	2	3	4	5

	No		Some		A lot
Do the activities help you understand?	1	2	3	4	5

	No		Some		A lot
Does the discussion help you understand?	1	2	3	4	5

	No		Some		A lot
Does the book help you understand?	1	2	3	4	5

	No		Some		A lot
Does the web material help you understand?	1	2	3	4	5

	No		Some		A lot
Do you see connections between the course material and the broader world?	1	2	3	4	5

What aspect of the course most helps you to learn?

What aspect of the course do you find most difficult?

Do you have any suggestions for things the course could include or emphasize to help you better learn?

Information Sheet for Instructor

Name_____ Class Level_____

Phone _____   email_____

Major and Concentration _____

What are some other communication classes you have taken, and where have you taken them?

What are your career objectives? What do you hope to gain from this course to meet those objectives?

Do you have any special concerns or questions about completing this course?

Do you understand the policies set forth in the syllabus? If you do and you agree to abide by them, please sign below. If you have any questions or concerns, please see your instructor as soon as possible.

_____   _____
Signature   Date

Note: Complete this form and give it to your instructor during the first week of classes.

Communication Research Style Manual:
A Short and Savvy Approach to Conducting Research

Lisa Sparks, P.h.D.
George Mason University

Bent Tree Press

Printed in the United States of America.

ISBN: 1-933005-07-6

Bent Tree Press

59 Damonte Ranch Parkway, #B284 • Reno, NV 89521

www.benttreepress.com

Address all correspondence and order information to the above address.

The development of this style manual stemmed from student demand for a concise and simple style manual for communication students and researchers. It has evolved over several years and has been influenced by many great scholars, educators, and friends. I am particularly grateful to mentor and friend Dr. Gus Friedrich, Rutgers University, who guided me through my first rough attempts at learning how to properly cite sources in APA style as a beginning graduate student many years ago! I would like to express my appreciation and acknowledgement to my graduate student Jeannie McPherson. I am grateful for her insightful suggestions and efforts to make this style guide as user friendly as possible for undergraduate, as well as beginning graduate, students! Appreciation and acknowledgement are also given to the students who have contributed their ideas and samples for future students working their way through the mysteries of research methodology, and to those who graciously helped in the creation of many of the activities.

TABLE OF CONTENTS

CHAPTER 1

Introduction

The purpose of this communication research style guide is to do just that — guide you through the process of learning to cite research properly! This is not meant to be a comprehensive communication research guide to citing sources. Rather, my goal is to provide a simple guide that really gets to the heart of what you need to cite your sources in communication research papers. You may be thinking, "Why do I have to cite my sources in a specific style?" There are several reference styles to choose from. However, when conducting communication research, you will most often use APA style. It is important to learn to follow an editorial style that scholars use most frequently, and since most (certainly not all) of the academic journals in communication require APA style, this communication research style manual primarily focuses on the nuts and bolts of using APA style in communication research! I have tried to touch on key problem areas students and beginning-level researchers are likely to encounter by going over how to locate sources of research, how to critically evaluate supporting materials, and how to follow APA style guide. I have also provided examples of some typical college-level research paper assignments, student activities and exercises, and sample outlines and papers. It is my fervent hope that this short and savvy guide will help you through your first round of communication research papers and beyond!

Locating Sources of Research

There are distinct differences among sources of research in terms of the quality and validity of the information presented. Primary source material, most commonly found in scholarly journals, consists of original research containing first-hand information about the research topic. Typically, the information presented in primary sources includes original research that has been conducted by scholars. This includes theoretical essays and critical reviews of previous research that has undergone a rigorous peer-review process in which other scholars from that field of study have examined the methods and claims of the research and deemed it to be valid and pertinent to the overall body of research. Scholarly journals provide the best supporting information and should be the first place you look when trying to locate sources of communication research.

Secondary sources of research consist of encyclopedias, textbooks, magazines, newspapers, Web sites, newsletters, etc., and usually report on, or offer interpretations of, information gathered from primary sources. There is a risk that information used from secondary sources will be inaccurate and taint the research process since the materials are sometimes written by novices and can include opinions or misrepresentations that are either inadvertent or deliberate. In the research process, it is best to avoid secondary sources, or use them very minimally with a very critical eye.

The following example illustrates the differences between primary and secondary sources of communication information.

Example 1: Beatty and Behnke (1991) studied the effects of public speaking anxiety and the intensity of a speaking task on heart rate during performance. The authors report on and discuss the results of the study first hand in the academic journal *Human Communication Research*, making this a primary source because it comes straight from the authors.

However, the use of Beatty and Behnke's study as an illustration of effective use of observation methods by Frey, Botan and Kreps (2000) in the textbook *Investigating communication: An introduction to research methods* provides a secondary source because it is an interpretation of Beatty and Behnke's original study.

Scholarly Journals

Scholarly journals range in topic, length of articles, and frequency of publication. However, they all include peer-reviewed primary source articles. A list of scholarly communication and social scientific journals to consider when conducting communication research follows. When identifying articles to use in communication research, it is important to make sure that the article is focused on message exchange. So, at first glance, some of the journals below may seem out of place, but due to the interdisciplinary nature of communication, you can find articles focusing on communication issues in a variety of different publications. Additionally, professors are often good sources for identifying articles in specific areas of communication (e.g., mass, information technology, political, organizational, health, intercultural, instructional, interpersonal, etc.). Also check the reference sections of articles for additional sources to research. Many of these journals are available by subscription and are published by the associations discussed below. However, you can find them in most university libraries.

- *American Journalism Review*
- *Asian Journal of Communication*
- *Australian Journal of Communication*
- *Canadian Journal of Communication*
- *Columbia Journalism Review* .
- *Communication and Cognition*
- *Communication and the Law*
- *Communication Education*
- *Communication Monographs*
- *Communication Quarterly*
- *Communication Reports*
- *Communication Research*
- *Communication Research Reports*
- *Communication Review*
- *Communication Studies*
- *Communication Theory*
- *Communication Yearbook*
- *Critical Studies in Mass Communication*
- *Discourse and Society*
- *Discourse Processes*
- *European Journal of Communication*
- *Health and Social Work*
- *Health Communication*
- *Human Communication Research*
- *International Journal of Aging and Human Development*
- *Journal of Applied Communication Research*
- *Journal of the Association for Communication Administration*

- *Journal of Broadcasting and Electronic Media*
- *Journal of Business Communication*
- *Journal of Communication*
- *Journal of Communication Inquiry*
- *Journal of Development Communication*
- *Journal of Educational Television*
- *Journal of Cross Cultural Gerontology*
- *Journal(s) of Gerontology*
- *Journal of Health Communication*
- *Journal of Intercultural Communication*
- *Journal of International Communication*
- *Journal of Language and Social Psychology*
- *Journal of Marriage and the Family*
- *Journal of Mass Media Ethics*
- *Journal of Personal and Social Relationships*
- *Journal of Public Relations Research*
- *Journalism History*
- *Journal of Mass Communication Quarterly*
- *Language and Communication*
- *Management Communication Quarterly*
- *Mass Comm Review*
- *Mass Communication and Society*
- *Media & Methods*
- *Media, Culture & Society*
- *Media Studies Journal*
- *National Forensics Journal*
- *Newspaper Research Journal*
- *Philosophy and Rhetoric*
- *Political Communication*
- *Public Relations Review*
- *Quarterly Journal of Speech*
- *Qualitative Research Reports*
- *Research in Language and Social Interaction*
- *Rhetoric Review*
- *Southern Communication*
- *Southern Speech Communication Journal*
- *Studies in Communication*
- *The Gerontologist*
- *Western Journal of Communication*
- *Western Journal of Speech Communication*
- *World Communication*
- *Written Communication*

On-line Resources
There are many on-line databases and indexes that provide citations, abstracts and, sometimes, even full articles. The databases can usually be accessed via university libraries and through membership in professional communication associations. Many students and researchers begin their search for supporting articles in on-line databases. They provide easy accessibility and can provide a good indication of the amount and variety of research available pertaining to an area of interest. Here is a list of on-line communication and social science resources to consider:

- *Communication Abstracts*
- *CommIndex*
- *Comm Search*
- *Infotrac*
- *Lexis Nexis*
- *ProQuest*
- *PsycINFO*
- *Sociological Abstracts*

In addition to the on-line resources discussed above, researchers and students can also join professional organizations, which commonly host conferences where professionals, students, and scholars convene to network, report on research findings, and discuss trends in their fields. Many communication associations publish journals and indexes to help locate research articles. Below is a list of professional communication associations you may want to consider joining:

- **American Communication Association** — http://www.uark.edu/~aca/
- **Association for Women in Communication & Technology** — www.womcom.org
- **Center for Nonverbal Studies** — www.members.aol.com/nonverbal2
- **Central States Communication Association** — www.csca-net.org
- **Eastern Communication Association** — www.ecasite.org
- **International Communication Association** — www.icahdq.org
- **National Communication Association** — www.natcom.org
- **Public Relations Society of America** — www.prsa.org
- **Southern States Communication Association** — www.ssca.net
- **Western States Communication Association** — www.westcomm.org
- **World Communication Association** — http://facstaff.uww.edu/wca/Home.htm

CHAPTER 2

Critical Evaluation of Supporting Materials

Guidelines for Credible Source Material

With the overwhelming amount of information currently available via the Internet, television and print media, evaluating research sources can be a complex task. The credibility of an entire study depends upon the reliability of the information used to form the foundation of the study. As we have previously discussed, primary sources, such as research articles in scholarly journals, provide the best supporting evidence. However, there may be instances when other information, such as interviews and personal observations, prove to be valid sources. These types of qualitative data must be critically evaluated based on the merits of the authority and the methods used to collect the data before you decide whether to use it in your scholarly research. It is up to authors to decide which supporting materials will help their arguments. However, authors have an ethical obligation to make sure their supporting materials provide the most accurate and up-to-date information. Due to time constraints, it is impossible to expect any author to review every single source available on a given topic. However, the sources discussed in the preceding chapter provide many launching points for researchers and students to collect comprehensive samples of research on a topic. Using them will ensure valid and reliable study results.

Once sources are located, there are many questions authors must ask when deciding whether or not to include the supporting information. The following guidelines will acquaint you with appropriate methods for evaluating the appropriateness and validity of information. If you are unsure about the credibility or reliability of any secondary source, it is best not to use it to support your research.

1. **Is the information applicable to my research topic?**
   The first question an author should ask him- or herself when evaluating a source is: *Is this relevant to my argument?* Inexperienced researchers often employ easily accessible sources, rather than the most appropriate. Simply blending together a bunch of sources that have marginal relevance to the research topic might give the appearance of a well-supported study, but closer evaluation will likely uncover a disorganized and ineffective paper in translating and communicating your message to the reader. It is always best to use a few quality sources to support your rationale or arguments rather than using a great number of non-related sources that bury your message.

2. Does the author of the source have authority in the field, and is he or she published in other scholarly journals (i.e., is the author credible)?

Like any other source, the authority of the author helps determine the value of the information. Whether presented in a primary or secondary source, if an author is a well-known and well-published scholar in the field under discussion, it is safer to assume his or her arguments are more credible than, say, your friend Carlo.

3. Is the information current?

In most social sciences, and certainly in communication, it is always best to use the most up-to-date information available on any given topic. There are certain instances when important theories or pivotal research will have to be discussed. In these cases, the author would want to include these articles, no matter how far back they date. For instance, when doing a study involving Communication Apprehension, the researcher would definitely want to include information from James McCroskey's work in the 1970s, as well as any current articles on the topic. However, a general rule is that the more current the information, the better it will support your claims. The overarching assumption is that current articles will generally include key citations, and the reader most certainly will have read the original source.

4. Is the information clearly presented and verifiable? Is it backed by scholarly sources with a list of references?

As we previously discussed, using primary sources in research is optimal. This ensures that the information presented has undergone rigorous review by other scholars and has been found to be credible. Sometimes, information from secondary sources, such as the Web, is acceptable, as long as the author is able to clearly assess its validity and authorship. Additionally, the type of publication in which the information/study appears can also provide clues about the credibility of the source. Popular magazines, newspapers, and television are generally poor sources of information and should not be included in college-level papers as supporting evidence.

Web Evaluations

In addition to asking the questions above, Web-based resources call for additional points of evaluation. Web sites serve different purposes. There are several categories of Web sites, all of which can include reliable and unreliable information. A personal Web site, expressing the interests and biases of its author, can be a legitimate source, if the Web site owner is honest about his or her identity and is a credible source. Be extremely wary of sites that publish unsupported information. If the information is not a personal viewpoint, does the author tell you the original source? Is the original source credible? Web sites can be presented as one type of site, but may have a hidden agenda. Any group can give itself an official-sounding name or logo. Therefore, it is vital for researchers and students to develop a critical eye when evaluating the credibility of Internet sources. If you are not sure and have not had a chance to ask your instructor, then remember this: *When in doubt, throw it out!*

Although many search engines rank material according to their interpretation of what is relevant, that doesn't mean the material is relevant to your study or is reliable. If you are unsure about the source, credibility, or reliability of any Web source, it is best not to use it to support your research. Again, *When in doubt, throw it out!*

Types of Web Sites:
- **Personal Home Pages** — maintained by individuals. They are often informal. Individuals can post their resumes, links to favorite sites, and/or showcase their interests and ideas. Some personal Web sites also serve as professional sites. For example, many professors publish their syllabi, course material and, in some cases, their scholarship, on their personal Web pages. Entrepreneurs often advertise their services on home pages.

- **Special Interest Sites** — maintained by non-profit organizations or activists dealing with special issues, such as environmental concerns, political advocacy, etc. They can be relatively mainstream or radical in interests and vary widely in credibility of information. Special interest sites are, by their nature, biased. When using such sources, your readers should be aware of the source's special interest.

- **Professional Sites** — maintained by institutions/organizations, sometimes by individuals. They can include research, reference sources, and fact sheets. Many institutions provide such services to the public. The credibility of the institution or professional credential of the individual providing the facts gives clues as to the reliability of the information. Is the site just linking to sources? If so, the credibility of the information is connected to the originating sites.

- **News and Journalistic Sites and Blogs** — include national, international news, on-line newspapers, magazines, and "homegrown" Web publications. Anyone can publish his or her own "news" on the Web. What do you know about, or what can you find out about, the reputation of the periodical? Is it an electronic version of a credible print publication? Remember, just because information is published does not necessarily mean it is true. If a periodical article has an ISSN number (International Standard Serial Number), it will probably have more authority.

- **Commercial Sites** — Although many legitimate businesses have Web sites, some are not legitimate. Companies with good and bad reputations are in the business of making money and acquiring and keeping customers. They are naturally biased in favor of their own products, so watch out for inflated claims of performance and quality. Companies will not showcase their competitors' products. If you are, for example, comparing products, get impartial reviews, not company information.

Plagiarism

Plagiarism is representing another's work as your own (see e.g., www.turnitin.com). If you like an author's ideas and want to include them in your paper, that is okay, as long as you cite the author! You will need to completely rewrite his or her idea into your own words AND cite the author and the year. If you take his or her exact words, you will have to cite the author's paper, along with the exact page number and the year it was published. However, it is important to note that whenever possible, it is best to rewrite the ideas and thoughts into your own words, rather than to use a direct quotation. Beginning writers tend to use too many direct quotations. More advanced writers learn the art of rewriting the salient ideas into their own words, while still citing the relevant sources!

Now that we are on the topic of citing relevant sources, you may be thinking about the best way to do just that (especially if you are writing your first social scientific-oriented paper)! When conducting research, it is necessary to cite sources of information and ideas throughout your paper. There are specific APA guidelines to guide you in making sure that all sources cited in your research are given proper credit. With technology in the twenty-first century, it is easy to cut and paste others' work. But, remember: if you don't cite it, it is plagiarism, and you are plagiarizing! Remember to use proper source citations in citing the evidence, ideas, and quotations you use in your work. The next chapter provides detailed examples of different situations often encountered when developing a research paper, and outlines the proper methods for citing others' work in APA 5th edition style.

CHAPTER 3

A Concise APA Style Guide

When you use someone else's words or ideas in a speech or a paper, you must provide information that identifies the source of that information. If you paraphrase or quote the person directly, you must identify the author. There are several reference styles to choose from. However, when conducting communication research, you will most often use APA style. If you have further questions after reading this chapter, see the *Publication Manual of the American Psychological Association 5th ed.*, or ask your instructor, and/or see http://www.apastyle.org.

A Note about Terms

Your instructor will refer to identifying the sources of the information you use in your written assignments and speeches in a variety of ways. *To reference, to document, to give credit to*, and *to cite* all mean the same thing — identifying the origin of ideas, writing, and information you use in your own writing and speeches. A *reference* and a *citation* are the same, but they appear in two forms. The first form occurs within the body of your paper, outline, or speech and may be a direct acknowledgement, such as, "In 2005, Gary Kreps wrote about…", or it may be a parenthetical reference or citation, e.g., (Kreps, 2005). The *in-text* citation corresponds to the second form, which appears at the end of your paper, as a complete reference in a list of references that appears on its own page, titled simply, **References** (not "Works Cited" or "Bibliography").

Citing References in Text

One Work by a Single Author (direct quotation)
In 2006 Harwood stated, "intergroup processes are important for..." (p. 68).
Harwood claims, "intergroup processes are important for..." (2006, p. 68).
Harwood (2006) points out, "intergroup processes are important for..." (p. 68).

One Work by a Single Author (paraphrased information)
Harwood (2006) compared intergroup processes…
In a recent study of intergroup processes (Harwood, 2006)…
In 2006, Harwood compared …
In a recent study of intergroup processes, Harwood (2006) described the method…

One Work by Multiple Authors
Join the names in a multiple-author citation in running text by the word "and." For example, Harwood and Sparks (2003) state that health and social identity can greatly impact an individual's health choices. In parenthetical material, in tables and in the reference list, join the names with an ampersand (&) (Harwood & Sparks, 2003). In sum, remember to use an ampersand within parentheses and the word "and" outside of parentheses.

> **Example 1 (two authors):**
> Harwood and Sparks (2003) found … [omit year from subsequent citations after first citation within a paragraph]

> **Example 2 (three or more authors):**
> Rowan, Sparks, Pecchioni, and Villagran (2003) found … [first citation in text should always list all of the contributing authors' names]
> Rowan et al. (2003) found [subsequent citations of the same reference need only list the first author's name followed by et al. and the year published. If cited again in the same paragraph, omit the year.]
> It is also important to note that you should have three or more authors in order to use the et al. rule.

Authors Cited in the Work of Another Author
Give credit to the original source and to the source you actually used:
> Weber (as cited in McCroskey, 2005), found that most college students…

Groups as Authors
> Example of citing a group author (e.g., an association, or government agency) is readily identified by its abbreviation.

Entry in Reference List:
> National Institute of Mental Health. (2005). *Antidepressant medications for children and adolescents: Information for parents and caregivers*. Retrieved on April 17, 2005, from www.nimh.nih.gov/healthinformation/antidepressant_child.cfm.

> **First text citation:**
> (National Institute of Mental Health [NIMH], 2005)

> **Subsequent text citations:**
> (NIMH, 2005)

> **Example of Citing a Group Author in Full**
> The National Institute of Mental Health (2005) claims that depression is a serious disorder that can cause significant problems in mood, thinking, and behavior at home, in school, and with peers. It is estimated that major depressive disorder (MDD) affects about 5 percent of adolescents, who have more frequent suicidal thinking and behavior and greater likelihood of substance abuse than youth in general (NIMH, 2005). However, research has shown that depression in children and adolescents can be treated with medication and certain types of psychological therapies, but still, knowledge of antidepressant treatments in youth remains limited when compared with what is known about treatment of depression in adults (NIMH).

Works with No Author (Including Legal Materials) or with an Anonymous Author

When a work has no author, cite in-text the first few words of the reference list entry (usually the title) and the year. Use double quotation marks around the title of an article or chapter, and italicize the title of a periodical, book, brochure, or report:
> on free care ("Study Finds," 2006)
> the book *College Bound Seniors* (2006)

When a work's author is designated as "Anonymous," cite in-text the word "Anonymous," followed by a comma and the date:

(Anonymous, 2007)

Personal Communication (e.g., e-mail, discussion, groups, telephone conversations)

Because they do not provide recoverable data, personal communications are not included in the reference list. Cite personal communication in-text only. Give the initials, as well as the surname of the communicator, and provide as exact a date as possible:

L. Sparks (personal communication, October 18, 2006)

Citing a List of References

There are several different sources for references that all appear uniquely within the references section. Follow these instructions when entering references into the references list.

Basic Rules for References
- Double-space all lines and entries.
- Do not number entries. Rather, put the entries in alphabetical order by author or article title.
- The second line and all subsequent lines in a reference entry should be indented — also known as hanging indent.

Citing Volume and Issue Numbers for References
Following are several examples of references to periodicals, which can sometimes be confusing in terms of proper citation style. Look at the difference in the next two examples:

Sparks, L., Kreps, G. L., Botan, C., & Rowan, K. (2005). Responding to terrorism: Translating communication research into practice. *Communication Research Reports, 22,* 1-5.

Wooten, P. (1993). Making humor work. *Journal of Nursing Jocularity, 3*(4), 46-47.

As you notice, the first citation only indicates the volume number 22, whereas the second citation provides both the volume number 3 and the issue number (4). The reason for the discrepancy is that some journals number the pages starting with 1 at the beginning of every issue, so that in a given volume, you may have several papers that begin with the same page number. When this is the case, APA style requires that you indicate the number of the issue so that the paper can be properly accessed. On the other hand, when the page numbering begins with 1 at the beginning of the volume and continues throughout the entire volume, then the APA style requires that you only indicate the volume number because there is no danger of confusion when retrieving a specific article.

Referencing Several Works from the Same Author
Arrange by year of publication with the earliest year first (e.g., list years from earliest to latest):

Example 1:

Wanzer, M. B., Booth-Butterfield, M. & Booth-Butterfield, S. (1995). The funny people: A source-orientation to the communication of humor. *Communication Quarterly, 43,* 142-154.

Wanzer, M. B., Booth-Butterfield, M. & Booth-Butterfield, S. (1996). Are funny people popular? An examination of humor orientation, loneliness, and social attraction. *Communication Quarterly, 44,* 42-52.

Wanzer, M. B., Booth-Butterfield, M. & Booth-Butterfield, S. (2005). "If we didn't use humor, we'd cry": Humorous coping communication in health care settings. *Journal of Health Communication, 10,* 105-125.

Wanzer, M. B., Frymier, A. B., & Sparks, L. (2005, November). An exploration of the relationship between humor, coping efficacy, and life satisfaction for older adults. Paper presented at the meeting of the National Communication Association, Boston, MA.

Example 2:
Wooten, P. (1993). Making humor work. *Journal of Nursing Jocularity, 3*(4), 46-47.
Wooten, P. (1996a). *Compassionate laughter: Jest for the health of it.* Salt Lake City, UT: Commune-A-Key.
Wooten, P. (1996b). Humor: An antidote for stress. *Holistic Nursing Practice, 10*(2), 49-56.

Example 3:
Gudykunst, W. B. (1995). Anxiety/uncertainty management (AUM) theory: Current status. In R. L. Wiseman (Eds.). *Intercultural communication theory* (pp. 8-58). Thousand Oaks, CA: Sage.
Gudykunst, W. B. (2004). An Anxiety/Uncertainty Management (AUM) theory of effective communication: Making the mesh of the net finer. In W. B. Gudykunst (Eds.). *Theorizing about communication and culture.* Thousand Oaks, CA: Sage.

One-author Entries are Listed before Multiple-author Entries with the Same Name.
Gudykunst, W. B. & Hammer, M. R. (1987). The influence of ethnicity, gender, and dyadic composition on uncertainty reduction in initial interactions. *Journal of Black Studies, 18*(2), 191-214.

Multiple-author Entries with the Same First Author are Arranged Alphabetically According to the Second Author.
Gudykunst, W. B., & Hammer, M. R. (1988). The influence of social identity and intimacy of interethnic relationships on uncertainty reduction processes. *Human Communication Research, 14,* 569-601.
Gudykunst, W. B., & Kim, Y. Y. (1997). *Communicating with strangers: An approach to intercultural communication.* New York, NY: McGraw-Hill.
Gudykunst, W. B., & Nishida, T. (1994). *Bridging Japanese/North American differences.* Thousand Oaks, CA: Sage.

References with the Same Multiple-authors Listed in the Same Order are Listed According to Year.
Gudykunst, W. B., & Hammer, M. R. (1987). The influence of ethnicity, gender, and dyadic composition on uncertainty reduction in initial interactions. *Journal of Black Studies, 18*(2), 191-214.
Gudykunst, W. B., & Hammer, M. R. (1988). The influence of social identity and intimacy of interethnic relationships on uncertainty reduction processes. *Human Communication Research, 14,* 569-60.

Examples of Citing Scholarly Works

Book
O'Hair, H. D., Sparks, L., & Kreps, G. L. (Eds.). (in press). *Handbook of communication and cancer care.* Cresskill, NJ: Hampton Press.
Smith, R. C., & Seltzer, R. (1992). *Race, class and culture.* Albany, NY: State University of New York Press.

Chapter from an Edited Book
Kreps, G. L., Alibek, K., Bailey, C., Neuhauser, L., Rowan, K., & Sparks, L. (2005). Emergency/risk communication to promote public health and respond to biological threats. In M. Haider (Ed.), *Global public health communication: Challenges, perspectives, and strategies* (pp. 349-362). Sudbury, MA: Jones and Bartlett Publishers.

Journal Article
Sparks, L., Kreps, G. L., Botan, C., & Rowan, K. (2005). Responding to terrorism: Translating communication research into practice. *Communication Research Reports, 22,* 1-5.

Journal Article in Press
Pecchioni, L., & Sparks, L. (in press). Health information sources of individuals with cancer and their family members. *Health Communication.*

Entire Issue or Special Section of a Journal

Sparks, L., Kreps, G. L., Botan, C., & Rowan, K. (Eds.). (2005). Communication and terrorism [Special Issue]. *Communication Research Reports, 22*(1).

Movie

Scorsese, M. (Producer), & Lonergan, K. (Writer/Director). (2000). *You can count on me* [Motion picture]. United States: Paramount Pictures.

Film, Limited Circulation

Harrison, J. (Producer), & Schiechen, R. (Director). (1992). *Changing our minds: The story of Evelyn Hooker* [Film]. 170 West End Avenue, Suite 25R, New York, NY, 10023: Changing our Minds, Inc.

Television Broadcast

Crystal, L. (Executive Producer). (1993, October 11). *The MacNeil/Lehrer news hour.* New York and Washington, DC: Public Broadcasting Service.

Television Series

Miller, R. (Producer). (1989). *The mind*. New York: WNET.

Single Episode from a Television Series

Restak, R. M. (1989). Depression and mood (D. Sage, Director). In J. Sameth (Producer), *The mind*. New York: WNET.

Magazines and Newspapers

Garner, H. (1981, December). Do babies sing a universal song? *Psychology Today*, pp. 70-76. Study finds free care used more. (1982, April 10). *The New York Times*, p. A14.

Interviews

Interviewee's name. (Interview Date). Interviewee's title, affiliated organization. Type of interview. Phone number or address.

Kramer, N. J. (1993, May 15). Marketing Director, California State Railroad Museum. (916) 445-1234.

Report from the Government Printing Office (GPO)

National Institute of Mental Health. (1982). *Television and behavior: Ten years of scientific progress and implications for the eighties* (DHHS Publication No. ADM-821195). Washington, D.C.: US Government Printing Office.

Report from Private Organization, Corporate Author & Publisher

Life Insurance Marketing Association. (1978). *Profits and the AIB in United States ordinary companies* (Research Report No. 1978-6). Hartford, CT: Author.

On-Line/Internet/Electronic Media

FTP

Sparks, L. (2006). *The life and times of the Sparks family.* Retrieved May 8, 2007, from ftp://yaddayadda.gmu.edu/pub/ Sparks File: comm.02.3.11.family.33.Sparks.

World Wide Web Page
    The components of a URL are as follows (see www.apastyle.org)

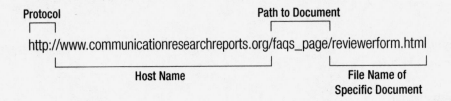

Pritzker, T. J. (n.d.). *An early fragment from central Nepal.* Retrieved November 7, 1997, from http://www.ingress. com/-astanart/pritzker.html.

Sparks, L. (2006). *The life and times of the Sparks family.* Retrieved April 22, 2006, from http://www.gmu.edu/depart-ments/comm/lsparks.html.

Internet Articles Based on a Print Source

Blow, J., & Off, M. (2006). The role of communication and letting off steam [Electronic version]. *Journal of Ventilation Research, 4,* 219-229.

Document Available on University Program or Department Web Site

Sparks, L. (2005). Presentation technology: What is effective and ineffective? Retrieved October 18, 2006 from George Mason University, Department of Communication Web site: http://www.gmu.edu/departments/comm/publica-tions/papers/sparks.html.

Other Examples

Oxford English dictionary. Retrieved 1992 from *Oxford UP, 2e, CD-ROM.*

McLuhan, M. (1972). We are all intertwingled. *Princeton Neologistic Review, 2,* 23-25. Retrieved November 7, 2003, from ProQuest database.

On-line Newspaper Article

Howell, V., & Carlton, B. (1993, August 29). Growing up tough: New generation fights for its life: Inner-city youths live by rule of vengeance. *Birmingham News,* p. 1A (10 pp.). Retrieved November 7, 2003, from Lexis/Nexis database.

Sample List of References

Adelman, R., & Greene, M. (2000). Communication between older patients and their physicians. *Clinics in Geriatric Medicine, 16,* 1-24.

Berg, S. (1996). Aging, behavior, and terminal decline. In J. E. Birren & K. W. Schaie (Eds.), *Handbook of the psychol-ogy of aging* (4th ed., pp. 323-337). San Diego, CA: Academic Press.

Booth-Butterfield, M. (2003). Embedded health behaviors from adolescence to adulthood: The impact of tobacco. *Health Communication, 15,* 171-185.

Chase, W., & Simon, H. (1973). The mind's eye in chess. In W. G. Chase (Ed.), *Visual information processing* (pp. 215-281). New York: Academic Press.

Harwood, J., & Sparks, L. (2003). Social identity and health: An intergroup communication approach to cancer. *Health Communication, 15,* 145-170.

Hutchinson, J., & Beasley, D. (1981). Speech and language functioning among the aging. In H. Oyer & E. Oyer (Eds.), *Aging and communication* (pp. 155-174). Baltimore: University Park Press.

Lapinski, M. K., & Levine, T. R. (2000). Culture and manipulation theory: the effects of self-construal and locus of benefit on information manipulation. *Communication Studies, 51,* 55-73.

Miller, R. (Producer). (1989). *The mind.* New York: WNET.

National Institute of Mental Health. (1982). *Television and behavior: Ten years of scientific progress and implications for the eighties* (DHHS Publication No. ADM-821195). Washington, D.C.: US Government Printing Office.

Nussbaum, J. F., Pecchioni, L., Robinson, J. D., & Thompson, T. (2000). *Communication and aging* (2nd). Mahwah, NJ: Lawrence Erlbaum Associates, Inc.

Pecchioni, L., Ota, H., & Sparks, L. (2004). Cultural issues in communication and aging. In Nussbaum, J. F., & Coupland, J. (Eds.), *Handbook of communication and aging research,* (pp. 167-207). Mahwah, NJ: Erlbaum.

Pritzker, T. J. (n.d.). *An early fragment from central Nepal.* Retrieved November 7, 1997, from http://www.ingress.com/-astanart/pritzker.html.

Rowan, K., Sparks, L., Pecchioni, L., & Villagran, M. (2003). The CAUSE model: A research supported aid for physicians communicating about cancer risk. *Health Communication, 15,* 239-252.

Sparks, L. (Ed.). (2003). Cancer communication and aging [Special Issue]. *Health Communication, 15*(2). 123-258.

Sparks, L., Kreps, G. L., Botan, C., & Rowan, K. (2005). Responding to terrorism: Translating communication research into practice. *Communication Research Reports, 22,* 1-5.

Wellman, B., & Gulia, M. (1999). Net surfers don't ride alone: Virtual communities as communities. In M. A. Smith & P. Kollock (Eds.), *Communities in cyberspace* (pp. 167-194). London: Routledge.

Headings and Series

Headings establish a format for your paper that readers can follow. The assignments outlined in Chapter Four refer to several sections in each description; the abstract, introduction, review of literature, methodology, results, discussion, and references, to name a few. In organizing your paper, it is important to note the main sections and subsections by using appropriate headings. Main section headings would include the previously listed sections. These would appear in regular roman text, centered directly above the top of the new section, as indicated in the Appendix A, B, C, D, and E examples. Subheadings are used to indicate main ideas within a main section (see Appendix D). They are flushed left and written in italicized roman-style font. Writers should avoid having only one sub-section, and therefore, one sub-section heading, within a main section. If additional headings are needed within the sub-section, a third level heading should be indented five spaces from the left and italicized. In sum, articles using APA style can have one to five levels of headings, but most authors use two or three levels.

Two levels:

Health Communication across the Life Span

Health and Younger Adults
Health and Older Adults

Three levels:

Health Communication across the Life Span

Health and Younger Adults
    Young adults.
    Middle-aged adults.

Health and Older Adults
    Younger-old.
    Older-old.

Appendices and Tables

All appendices should be cited within the body of your paper and then attached to the end of the paper in an Appendix section. Each appendix should begin on a new page and be labeled by placing a heading that reads "Appendix A" at the top center of each appendix. All proceeding appendices should be labeled B, C, D, and so on (See Appendices D and E at the end of this guide).

Tables should be numbered with Arabic numerals in the order in which the tables are mentioned within the text. Each table should have a brief but explanatory title that that appears to the top left of the table.

Example 1:

Table 1

All participants' ratings and statistical groupings of importance of health information sources.

Information Source	Importance mean (sd) *n*	Group Membership
Doctor	4.64 (.87) *166*	A
Family	4.03 (1.27) *147*	B
Nurse	3.88 (1.28) *156*	B, C
Flyers	3.63 (1.14) *152*	C, D
Friends	3.49 (1.37) *140*	D, E
Internet	3.49 (1.33) *146*	D, E
Television	2.69 (1.10) *143*	F

Example 2:

Table 1

Intercorrelations among empathy, affective orientation, identification, and frequency of exposure.

	1	2	3	4	5	6	7	8
1 Perspective Taking	—	—						
2 Emotional Contagion	.18*	—	—					
3 Empathic Concern	.39*	.41*	—	—				
4 Affective Orientation	.05	.29*	.30*	—	—			
5 Cognitive-Emotional ID	.16*	.11	.14*	.23*	—	—		
6 Similarity ID	.05	-.03	.03	.14*	.60*	—	—	
7 Group ID	.20*	.04	.09	.23*	.50*	.59*	—	—
8 Frequency of Exposure	-.11	-.09	-.07	.01	-.06	-.08	-.07	—

*p < .05

Example 1, Table 1 is derived from:

Pecchioni, L., & Sparks, L. (in press). Health information sources of individuals with cancer and their family members. *Health Communication*.

Example 2, Table 1 is derived from:

Chory-Assad, R. M., & Chicchirillo, V. (in press). Empathy and affective orientation as predictors of identification with television characters. *Communication Research Reports, 22*.

Spacing and Punctuation

When using APA style, every line in the paper should be double-spaced. Additionally, there should always only be one space after each punctuation mark and between each word. This is unlike MLA style that mandates two spaces after every period.

CHAPTER 4

College-Level Research Assignments

In communication studies there are specialized writing assignments that adhere to specific guidelines. The following section provides a brief description of six common writing assignments: a speech outline; an annotated bibliography; a literature review; a research prospectus; a research project; and a research article critique, and the guidelines of APA style that must be adhered to in developing these assignments.

Communication Research Approaches

In communication research there are two common approaches to understanding human communication behavior: qualitative and quantitative. To effectively study communication, students must understand the basic differences between these approaches to research.

Qualitative

The qualitative research approach focuses on the experiences, interpretations, impressions or motivations of research participants, and seeks to describe how people view things and why. It relates to beliefs, attitudes and changing behaviors of society as a whole, but usually deals with smaller subgroups of a population. Therefore, qualitative research can provide rich, thick, and subtle nuances in describing and interpreting the subgroups examined, but cannot be generalized to a larger population.

In qualitative research, it is thought that the researcher can learn the most about a situation by participating and/or being immersed in it; studying communication in a natural environment, rather than in a laboratory. Data is produced through this technique by using non-statistical procedures, such as in-depth interviews, review of documents and artifacts, researcher observations and participant observations that traditionally do not have a quantifiable value attached. For example, phenomenology, ethnography, conversation analysis, and discourse analysis are examples of tools used in qualitative design. In sum, qualitative research describes phenomena with words instead of numbers or measures. This approach provides researchers with a process-oriented research technique that is used to gain insight into the underlying issues surrounding a research problem by becoming personally involved in the data-gathering process. Van Maanen (1988) explains the difference nicely: quantitative research shows what is likely to happen when you mix various ingredients together, while qualitative research takes you into the kitchen to see the meal as it is being made.

Quantitative

In quantitative research designs, on the other hand, data is usually gathered using more structured research instruments, such as surveys. The researcher is ideally an objective observer who neither participates in nor influences what is being studied. The results provide less detail on the subtle nuances of behaviors and attitudes, and focus more objectively on studying human communicative behavior by using statistics and numerical evidence and data. Additionally, quantitative data is usually based on larger samples (ideally, randomly selected) that are representative of the population, and can therefore be generalized to a larger population.

Quantitative research can be replicated or repeated, giving it higher reliability. However, most researchers acknowledge that combining both techniques in a study, called triangulation, can often produce the best, most comprehensive data. When designing research, it is important to identify which approach best answers the research questions you are investigating and understand that whichever research approach you choose will certainly have benefits and limitations.

General Trends in Comparing Qualitative vs. Quantitative Approaches

	Qualitative Research	Quantitative Research
Objective	• To gain an understanding of underlying reasons and motivations • To provide insights into the setting of a problem, generating ideas and/or hypotheses for later quantitative research • To uncover trends in thought and opinion	• To quantify data and generalize results from a sample to the population of interest • To measure the incidence of various views and opinions in a chosen sample
Sample	• Often a small number that is non-representative of the larger population • Respondents selected to fulfill a given quota	• Usually a large number representing the population of interest • Randomly selected respondents
Data Collection	• Unstructured or semi-structured techniques, e.g., individual in-depth interviews, group discussions, observation	• Structured techniques, such as surveys
Data Analysis	• Non-statistical	• Statistical; data is usually in the form of tabulations • Findings are conclusive and usually descriptive in nature
Outcome	• Exploratory and/or investigative. Findings are not conclusive and cannot be used to make generalizations about the population of interest • Develop an initial understanding and sound base for further decision-making • Non-probabilistic	• Used to recommend a final course of action • 95% Probability of prediction(s) (95% certain the outcome is appropriately estimating the sample to the population of interest)

Examples of College-Level Research Assignments

In the following pages, I provide examples of typical college-level assignments you are likely to encounter. These examples reflect my personal biases and preferences. These assignments are meant to provide a starting point for different research-based assignments, but remember your instructor's approach is always the best one!

Speech Outline Assignment

Speech outlines provide a way to organize your ideas logically and clearly, and can also serve as a speaking script. They usually are two to four pages, but can vary in length, depending on instructor requirements. While there are a variety of approaches to constructing speech outlines, a typical speech outline provides a detailed plan for any type of oral presentation. It consists of three major sections: an introduction, a body, and a conclusion (see Appendix A).

Introduction: Contains a greeting and attention-getter. Presents the main topic of the speech and tells the audience what major points your speech will make.

Body: Elaborates on the main points of your speech. This is where you focus on details and provide evidence to explain and support your points.

Conclusion: Summarizes the main points of your speech and stresses the most-important details to make a lasting impact on the audience.

- Each of the three previously discussed sections should have its own section heading, with each section beginning with the Roman numeral I, flushed all the way to the left margin.
- Beginning with the introduction section, list all of the major elements, including the attention-getter, a thesis statement specifying the purpose and intent of the speech, credibility statement, and a preview of the main elements, using Roman numerals to indicate each point. Indent information included under any of these subheadings and remember that if you subdivide a point, there must be at least two points, i.e., if there is an A, there must also be a B. This section ends with a transition statement (indicated in parentheses) that signals the end of the introduction and the beginning of the main part of the speech.
- The body section follows the introduction and outlines the major elements intended to support the thesis of your speech. The initial point should begin with Roman numeral I, flushed to the left margin, and all other main points should follow with corresponding Roman numerals. Any sub-points should be indented five spaces and identified with capital letters, A, B, C, and so on. Sub-sub-points should be indented ten spaces and identified with numbers. Any information from an external source must include a reference and explanation of applicability. This section ends with a transition statement (indicated in parentheses) that signals the end of the body and the beginning of the conclusion of the speech.
- Within the conclusion, there are usually two parts: a summary that restates the main points of the speech, indicated by Roman numeral I, and a closure statement or call to action, indicated by Roman numeral II.
- The reference section should appear as in any work, with "References" centered at the top of the page and an alphabetized listing of works cited in APA style.

Annotated Bibliography Assignment

A typical assignment may ask for ten or more annotated bibliographies on a particular topic. This would require an alphabetized list of citations to books, articles, and documents, with each citation appearing in APA style on a new page at the top, followed by an annotation — a brief (usually about 150 words) descriptive and evaluative paragraph providing some assessment of value or relevance of the article. The entire citation and annotation should be double-spaced.

The purpose of the annotation is to inform the reader of the relevance, accuracy, and quality of the sources cited. In this description, your job is to paraphrase or sum up the general ideas of the work. What is the point of the work? What argument is the author making? What are some examples the author uses to support his or her argument?

Depending on your assignment, an annotated bibliography may be one stage in a larger research project, or it may be an independent project standing on its own. An annotation briefly restates the main argument of a source. An annotation of an academic source, for example, typically identifies its thesis, research question, and/or hypothesis, its major methods of investigation, and its main conclusions. Keep in mind that identifying the argument of a source is a different task than describing or listing its contents. Rather than listing contents, an annotation should account for why the contents are there (see Appendix B).

Title Page

Each of the following college-level research paper assignments requires a title page. The title page is the first page of the manuscript. It contains the title of the paper, the authors' names, their institutional affiliations, and the running head. The title summarizes the main topic or key variables studied and should be about 10-12 words in length. Avoid unnecessary words in the title, such as "An Experimental Study of…" or "A Research Investigation…" Examples of suitable short titles would be "Teacher immediacy in the non-traditional classroom," or "The effect of a parent on the adult/child marital relationship." The author's or authors' name(s) are located below the title and the organizational affiliation is below the author's name. The title and names of the author and organizational affiliation should all be double-spaced and centered between the left and right margins on the upper half of the page. The running head is an abbreviation of the title. It is located on the upper left-hand side of the paper, below the header, and above the title. All letters are capitalized and the title should not exceed 50 typewritten characters, counting letters, punctuation, and spaces. Use the header function to insert the running head and a page number in the upper-right corner of each page.

Word Formatting Tip for Headers (aka: Running head)
To use the header function, follow the six steps below:

1. Select view from the top of your screen.
2. Select the "Header and Footer" function from the drop-down menu under view.
3. A header box will appear at the top of your paper. Select the insert auto text function from the upper left of your screen.
4. Select insert page number, and a page number will appear inside the header box. Flush the page number to the right and insert the running head before the page number so that it appears: Your Running Head 1 (e.g., Health Communication across the Life Span 1).
5. Every page should be numbered consecutively, starting with page 1 on your title page.
6. Once your running head is in place, click your mouse on the body of your paper and you will be able to resume typing.
7. Remember that your running head throughout the manuscript should be a subset of the running head you list on your title page.

Example of a Title Page

Running head: COMMUNICATION COMPETENCE

Communication Competence Among Health Care Providers

and Older Adult Consumers

Eager Learner

Hometown University

Example of a Title Page

Running head: EFFECTIVE COMMUNICATION

Effective Communication Among

Health Care Workers

John Smith

Any State University

Review of Literature Assignment

A review of literature is a summary and evaluation of what scholars and researchers have written on a topic (see Appendix C). It should be organized according to a guiding concept, such as your research objective, thesis, or the problem/issue you wish to address, and should give the reader a clear overview of existing data on a topic, and the methods used to glean that data.

Organizational Structure of a Review of Literature

The format of a review of literature consists of the following components:

1. Title page (see Title Page example)
2. Introduction
3. Statement of the problem/topic being investigated
4. Review of identified literature
5. Conclusion based on your findings and assessment
6. References

The objective of a review of literature is not to list as many articles as possible; rather, you want to demonstrate your intellectual ability to recognize relevant information, and to synthesize and evaluate it according to the guiding concept you have determined for yourself. Existent literature should be identified and evaluated using **information-seeking skills,** or the ability to scan the literature efficiently using manual or computerized methods to identify a set of potentially useful articles and books, and **critical appraisal,** or the ability to apply principles of analysis to identify those studies that are unbiased and valid. A literature review is NOT just a summary. It is an organized synthesis of the results of your search. It must **organize information** and relate it to the thesis or research question you are developing, **synthesize results** into a summary of what is and isn't known, **identify controversy** when it appears in the literature, and **develop questions** for further research.

Try to avoid beginning every paragraph of your review with the names of researchers. Instead, organize your review into useful, informative sections that present themes or identify trends. Some questions to ask when formulating a review of literature are

1. Do I have a specific thesis, problem, or research question that my literature review helps to define?
2. What is the scope of my literature review? How good are my information-seeking skills? Has my search been wide enough to ensure I've found all the relevant material? Has it been narrow enough to exclude irrelevant material? Is the number of sources I've used appropriate for the length of my paper?
3. Is there a specific relationship between the literature I've chosen to review and the problem I have formulated?
4. Have I critically analyzed the literature I use? Do I just list and summarize authors and articles, or do I assess them? Do I discuss the strengths and weaknesses of the cited material?
5. Have I cited and discussed studies contrary to my perspective?

Example of a Literature Review

Review of Literature

Recently, researchers have expanded the definition of ethnicity to also include identity and perceptions of others. Toale and McCroskey (2001) define ethnic identity as having a sense of belonging to, and having knowledge and shared experiences of, a particular group. This perception of belonging is what distinguishes the construct of ethnicity from the more biological term "race." Chen (2000) combines phenotypic characteristics and perceived identity to define ethnicity as being socially constructed by people who exclusively share cultural traits, ancestry, physical appearance, or a sense of social belonging or loyalty to a group.

While it is clear that strong arguments exist to represent people according to ethnic identity, for the purpose of this study, the author defines ethnicity according to the more traditional definition of skin color and physical attributes. Since this study will examine how ethnocentrism contributes to anxiety and uncertainty in initial interethnic communication with a stranger, the author believes that characteristics based on appearances, such as skin color and other physical traits, are more salient for discovering how respondents will react. This idea is supported by Khmelkov and Hallinan's (1999) study, which found that race is salient in interpersonal attraction, and Gudykunst (2004) who found that we tend to be attracted to strangers who appear similar to us. Specific races to be examined are African-American, Asian-American, Caucasian, Hispanic-American and Middle Eastern.

Communication Styles/Stereotypes

According to Toale and McCroskey (2001) an individual's ability to effectively communicate in interethnic conversations with strangers is largely dependent on psychological factors, such as his or her level of ethnocentrism, and perceptions held about other ethnic groups. Moreover, unique communication behaviors are employed by members of different ethnic groups and may inhibit effective interethnic communication (Toale & McCroskey, 2001; Lapinski & Levine, 2000; Hecht, Ribeau, & Alberts, 1989; Leonard & Locke, 1993). In order to communicate effectively, one must have an understanding of an interactant's customs and perceptions.

Communicative Differences Among Ethnic Groups

Hispanic-American people are often more comfortable than are European-American individuals when in close physical proximity to other people (Hall, 1990). Without this knowledge, a European-American person interacting with a Hispanic-American person may take the closeness as an inappropriate advance, while the Hispanic-American person may see the European-American person's distance as rude.

Research Project/Research Prospectus Assignment

The purpose of a research prospectus is to increase your organizational, analytical, writing, and research skills by completing an appropriate communication-based literature review, along with a methodological research strategy to test your created hypothesis and research questions. The assignment is typically between 4-6 typed pages, but can vary according to instructor preferences (see Appendix D). A research project entails carrying out the project outlined in a research prospectus (see Appendix E for a quantitative research project and Appendix F for a qualitative research project).

This assignment involves identifying a problem or issue, reviewing the literature on the problem, isolating one or more hypotheses and/or research questions, and outlining a research strategy or methodology to test the hypothesis(es) or answer the research question(s). The project should include, at a minimum, the following (See Appendices for examples):

- Title page in APA style.
- An abstract of your project (100-200 word brief summary).
- An introduction or justification for the research project studying specific phenomenon/a. Typically, the introduction will provide rationale for why your topic is worth studying, and the literature review supports your justification.
- A review of the literature (summary of previous findings on this and related issues); should comprise 65-70 percent of the paper.
- A clear statement of at least one hypothesis (research questions and more hypotheses are optional).
- A statement of the methodology you will use to test the hypothesis or answer the research question(s). This should include definitions of operationalized variables, populations and sampling, and the methodology.
- A clear identification of the statistic(s), if appropriate, and the specific variable measurement (nominal, ordinal, interval, ratio) you will use to compare/assess in testing the hypothesis proposed. The hypothesis should be derived from the prior literature with intent to carry out the next research step. HINT: Hypotheses should not magically appear depending on the way the wind might be blowing the day you are thinking about it; they must be based on prior research. Qualitative research sometimes has exceptions to this rule, due to its exploratory nature.
- A reference section with several properly cited sources in APA 5th edition style, the majority of which come from academic journals.
- Use third person, not first person in writing.
- Avoid passive voice.
- Stay gender neutral.

Organizational Structure of a Research Prospectus

Title page

Should always be page one of a research prospectus (see Title Page example)

Abstract

The abstract is a very concise summary of the entire paper, usually about 100-200 words in length. It appears on its own page, and the first paragraph is not indented. It should contain the purpose of your paper, organizing criteria, and conclusions based on your analysis. Because this is all of the report that most people are likely to read, it must be accurate, self-contained, and brief. Someone reading an abstract should be able to see at a glance what was studied, what was done, and what outcome was reached (See Appendix D, E and G for examples).

Introduction

The introduction tells the reader about the topic — what the issue is, what is known about it, and what your specific focus is. The introduction begins on a new page with the title of the article centered at the top. It contains a statement of the problem, its theoretical and practical significance, and its place in a larger body of knowledge. Begin the introduction with a paragraph clearly indicating the topic under study. Following the opening paragraph, present what is known on the topic in an effort to build your rationale for researching this important topic. Your introduction should be no more than a page.

Review of Literature

This is where you review existing literature related to your topic. In this section, you tell the reader what other researchers have found regarding your specific topic. Stick to the essentials, that is, previous findings that are directly pertinent to your study. This section should define the key variables and describe the purpose or rationale of what you did in your study, explain the purpose of the paper and the significance of the topic, and provide a brief background to orient the reader. This section sets the tone of the paper and includes specific research questions or hypotheses.

This section should
1. argue for the importance of studying this area,
2. briefly review previous findings in the area,
3. describe the purpose of the study and rationale for performing it,
4. present an argument for your specific expectations for the study,
5. close by presenting those expectations in the form of at least one specific hypothesis.

Formatting Research Questions and Hypotheses

In the body of a literature review, the first line and every subsequent line of the statement of a research question and/or hypotheses should always be indented once from the left. Additionally, an upper-case RQ or H, followed by a numerical indication of which research question or hypotheses it represents should appear.

Example:

Research Questions

RQ1: What is the role of ethnocentrism in initial interethnic communication?

RQ2: How does ethnocentrism impact anxiety/uncertainty management?

Hypothesis

H1: Individuals will report having more information regarding cancer after they or a family member has received a cancer diagnosis than before.

Remember, a review of literature should be the argument and the justification for why you are doing the study. It should not simply list descriptions of other studies, followed by a hypothesis. Search for models and examples of literature reviews in some scholarly peer-reviewed articles.

Tips for Structuring Hypotheses and/or Research Questions

Solid hypotheses and research questions should be based on prior literature and should clearly identify specific variables under investigation with some relationship, prediction, or interaction between or among variables. Variables should be properly and clearly operationalized and therefore _TESTABLE_! In quantitative research, you should be able to measure variables. In qualitative research, you should have a process for thoroughly and accurately recording observations.

- **BAD:** Different types of beer affect college students on certain tasks.
  (You should be asking yourself: Affect what? What type of tasks? Variables must be more clearly identified.)
- **BETTER:** Students exposed to one hour of drinking beer while studying will recall significantly less about the material than students exposed to one hour of drinking Dr. Pepper while studying.
- **BAD:** When women appear on television ads they are usually presented as homemakers.
- **BETTER:** Women appearing on television ads are significantly more likely than men to be presented as home-makers.

Tips and Tricks on Effective Citing

Paraphrase authors' work when possible, rather than using too many direct quotations.

- Avoid referring to article titles when introducing research. Professional reviews typically refer to authors' last names only.
  - **BAD:** Professor of Communication Melissa Wanzer, in her article entitled _Humor orientation, competency, and immediacy_, argues that...
  - **BETTER:** Wanzer (2006) argues that...

Try not to use full sentence quotations (e.g., an entire sentence). Instead, use transition phrases to introduce the quotation.

- **BAD:** "The process of selection implies that an individual's expectations are adjusted to permit the subjective experience of satisfaction as well as personal control" (Baltes & Baltes, 1990, p. 22).
- **BETTER:** Baltes and Baltes (1990) have proposed the principle of "selective optimization with compensation" to explain a "strategy of effective aging that allows for self-efficacy and growth in the context of increasing biological vulnerability and reduced reserve capacity" (p. 21).
- **BETTER:** Although it may be common to think that older adults feel much less positively about their lives because they can see how happy and healthy younger adults are, in reality, "older adults tend to orient their comparison standards toward old people in similar situations" (Baltes & Baltes, 1990, p. 19).

Methodology

This section should discuss your procedures in a clear, systematic, accurate, and comprehensive account. It identifies and describes criteria used for evaluation of the research article and describes what you did and how you did it. Other researchers should be able to repeat the study from the account provided. The details are described in sub-sections under appropriate headings. Most methods sections have several sub-sections, depending upon your type of study.

Participants

The participants are the respondents or subjects of the study: who was observed, who answered the interviewer's questions, or who filled out the survey. Give the number of individuals and describe the relevant characteristics, such as gender and age. For example, "Thirty-one men and 23 women students in the basic communication course at a large mid-Atlantic university filled out the questionnaire." Also describe how the sample was selected and the degree to which it represents the population of interest. For a content analysis of magazines or videos, a participant section is unnecessary.

Variables/Apparatus/Materials

Instrumentation or materials are described in this section, including observation sheets, questionnaires used, etc.

Setting

Observational studies often require a description of the setting in which the information was collected: for example, a description of the site or event where the study took place. This information might be combined with the section describing the research subjects.

Procedures/Data Analysis

Describe how the data are to be obtained. In addition to the actual data collection, this section would include information about training for interviewers or experimenters, a description of the physical setting in which the data are to be collected, instructions to the participants, and mention of any special problems that need to be addressed. Any pilot tests or reliability checks made on procedures or equipment used would also be described here. For a content analysis, describe the development and use of the coding categories.

References

STOP HERE FOR A RESEARCH PROSPECTUS

A full research project would go on to conduct the experiment or study outlined in the methodology section and report on the results. Additionally, a discussion of procedures and findings is always included in a complete research project.

Results

This is where you report on factual information about what was found. Opinions and interpretations are reserved for the discussion. Begin the section with the findings most relevant to the hypothesis or problem, then present any secondary or related findings. The presentation of results should follow the order of the hypotheses or questions raised in the introduction. Don't skip from Hypothesis 1 then back to 2. Let the reader know the results of each hypothesis before going on to the next.

Discussion

The discussion section describes what your findings mean in light of the information you presented in the introduction. This is your opportunity to interpret the findings, discuss their significance, and suggest directions for future research. Researchers typically open the discussion section with a clear statement about the answers to the questions raised in the introduction and describe support or nonsupport for the hypotheses. *IMPORTANT: There is no need to repeat everything that was said in the results. Instead, describe how your findings fit existing theories and other research in the field (the parts reviewed in the introduction). What general conclusions can you draw? Based on what you have learned, what issues should be investigated next? What are the flaws and limitations in your study? If you were to repeat the study, what would you change? In other words, the discussion fits your particular piece of research into the context that you established in the introduction. It completes the work at hand, which is to add new information or knowledge, and it points ahead to future research. In sum, the discussion is the interpretive segment of the paper and loops back to answer the issues raised in the introduction.*

References

Provide an alphabetized listing of all references cited in the prospectus. This section should always begin on a new page, and references should be double-spaced, with all lines following the first in the citation indented five spaces.

Word Formatting Tip for References

When constructing your references section, set your computer to the hanging indent function by following the five steps below. Once you have followed the instructions, your references should automatically indent all lines following the first in each citation by five spaces.

1. Select the format tool at the top of your screen.
2. Select the paragraph function.
3. In the indents and spacing section, select "hanging indent" under the "special" function.
4. Set the indent to occur at 0.25.
5. Select OK.

Research Article Critique Assignment

This assignment requires students to select and critique a published work of empirical research. The purpose of this assignment is to give the student an opportunity to demonstrate the ability to critically evaluate scholarly research. Such works are reports of original research that generally consist of descriptions of the distinct stages of the research effort. The article selected should, therefore, generally follow the sequence of stages previously described: introduction, review of literature, method, results, and discussion. The student is to use this assignment to apply knowledge gained regarding the roles of theory and research in explaining and predicting human communication.

A critique of an article requires identification of criteria on which to base an evaluation (see below). Students should clearly identify and explain the criteria used in assessing the research. After describing these criteria, examples from the article that illustrate how the article meets or fails to meet the standard criteria should be provided. In addition, an overall evaluation of the article regarding its contribution or lack of contribution to knowledge of the research problem should be provided.

Here are examples of appropriate criteria. The list is not exhaustive. The intent is to provide ideas for selecting criteria.

1. Adequacy of literature review.
2. Significance of the hypotheses or research question(s).
3. What variable(s) (if any) are being examined?
    a) What is/are the independent variable(s)?
    b) What is/are the dependent variable(s)?
4. Reliability of instruments.
5. Validity of instruments.
6. Appropriateness and explanation of research design.
7. Generalizability of findings.
8. Clarity of hypothesis or research question.
9. Explanation of operational definitions.
10. Methodological procedures used to gather and analyze data.
11. Adequate reporting of data-gathering procedures.
12. Presentation of results and conclusions drawn from the data (or results).
13. Ability to replicate.
14. Contribution to clarity of problem/theory.

Organizational Structure of a Research Critique

The format for the paper is similar to that of the research prospectus. It should include the title page, abstract, brief introduction, research criteria utilized, discussion, and reference list (see Appendix G). A brief description of each part follows.

Title Page

Should always be page one of a research critique (see Title Page example).

Abstract

The abstract should contain the purpose of your paper, organizing criteria, specific research criteria to be used in your analysis, and your discussion/conclusions based on your analysis. It appears on its own page, and the first paragraph is not indented. It is a 100-200 word concise summary of your entire paper. Someone reading an abstract should be able to see at a glance what was studied, what was done, and what outcome was reached. (See Appendices D, E and G for examples.)

Introduction/Review of Literature

The introduction begins on a new page, with the title of the article centered at the top. Begin the introduction/review of literature with a paragraph clearly indicating the topic under study. Provide a brief synopsis of the article you are critiquing and the purpose of your paper, including organizing criteria, specific research criteria to be utilized, and what will be discussed.

Defining Research Criteria

Clearly identify and define the research criteria within the article that you will be using to assess the research. After describing these criteria, provide examples from the article that illustrate how the article meets or fails to meet the standard criteria.

Critique/Discussion

Discuss and critique the article in terms of the research criteria chosen. Discuss the limitations of the study — what were problems in the design? This is an opportunity to show that you understand concepts and methods. Elaborate on what might be done in future research studies — what's the logical next step in research in this area? Be creative: There are no limits on studies you can suggest be done.

References

Provide an alphabetized listing of all references cited in the critique. References should primarily be used to support your definitions of research criteria chosen. This section should always begin on a new page, and references should be double-spaced, with all lines following the first in the citation indented five spaces.

Word Formatting Tip for References
When constructing your references section, set your computer to the hanging indent function by following the five steps below. Once you have followed the instructions, your references should automatically indent all lines following the first in each citation by five spaces.

1. Select the format tool at the top of your screen.
2. Select the paragraph function.
3. In the indents and spacing section, select "hanging indent" under the "special" function.
4. Set the indent to occur at 0.25.
5. Select OK.

CHAPTER FIVE

Student Activities and Exercises

Activity 1: Organizing a Speech to Inform

Purpose:

To help students understand the importance of organization.

Instructions:

Assume you are preparing an informative speech on the IDEAL WOMAN or MAN. Your task is to generate a brief outline — including a specific purpose statement, thesis statement, and three main points and sub-points. Be sure to identify the types of linear or configural organizational pattern you would use for this speech topic. (No research is needed for this assignment; just make up facts if you need to.)

Title:

Specific Purpose:

Thesis Statement:

Introduction:

       Attention-getter:

       Preview:

Body:
   I.
         A.
             a.
             b.
         B.
             a.
             b.
   II.
         A.
             a.
             b.
         B.
             a.
             b.
   III.
         A.
             a.
             b.
         B.
             a.
             b.

Conclusion:

Summary:

                    Memorable Statement

Activity 2: The Research Dimension: A Search into the Great Beyond

Objectives:
>To help students select substantive speech/research topics.
>To teach students how to narrow topics in order to make them more manageable.
>To expose students to library resources for researching their topics.

Directions:
>Choose a partner who will be able to conduct library research with you and with whom your schedule is compatible. Research and complete each of the following searches.

Author Search
>Find a book by Athena du Pre, Jake Harwood, Jon Nussbaum, Teresa Thompson, James McCroskey, Dan Nimmo, Melanie Booth-Butterfield, Steve Booth-Butterfield, Dan O'Hair, Gary Kreps, Howard Giles, Brant Burleson, Kevin Wright, or Michael Pfau.
>Write the call letters in this space._____

Use the proper bibliographic form to cite it by following this example.
Author's last name, first initial., middle initial. (date). *Title, in italics, with only the first word, proper nouns, and the first word of the subtitle capitalized.* City of publication: Company.

_____

_____

Subject Search
Book. Subject: health communication.
Call letters:_____
Cite properly, using the same pattern for citation as above:

_____

_____

Magazine or Journal Article
Subject: health communication or communication and aging. Follow this form to cite it:
Author(s)' last name, first initial., middle initial. (year, month [day]). Title capitalized same as above. *Magazine title in italics, volume in italics,* page number(s).

_____

_____

Newspaper Article
Subject: health or interpersonal communication. Follow this source citation format:
Author(s)' last name, first initial., middle initial. (year, month day). Title. *Newspaper title in italics,* p. number(s).

_____

_____

Electronically Stored Data
Find a television program on some health-related issue.
Last name, first initial., middle initial. (Producer), & last name, first initial., middle initial. (Director). (date). *Title in italics.* [Television program]. Company.

_____

_____

Internet
Find an article/summary on a recent political event.
Author. (year, month). *Title*. Retrieved on month date, year from, http://www.name of web site.com.

_____

_____

Reference Section
Write the title of the most unusual dictionary you can find. (Examples: New dictionary of Okie sayings; A dictionary of philosophy)

_____

_____

Activity 3: Supporting Materials (to cite sources)

Objective:

To understand the importance of using evidence to support claims.

To learn how to incorporate evidence into speeches and research.

Directions:

Students should choose a magazine article or advertisement that uses statistics to support a claim. Watch for the use of implied statistics without any numbers to back up the statistics (e.g., more doctors prefer drug A). Each student will have the opportunity to analyze the article and provide an explanation for the class:

1. What type of statistics are used in the article?

2. What claim are the statistics intended to support?

3. Does the article include information about the origin of the statistics (who did the research)?

4. Does the article effectively use the statistics to make an argument? Why or why not?

Activity 4: Managing Performance Anxiety — Presenting Research

PERSONAL REPORT OF PUBLIC SPEAKING ANXIETY (PRPSA)

You step up to the podium. Your heart is pounding. Your knees and hands are shaking. Your stomach has butterflies, and your mind seems completely blank. You can't get your visual aid to stand up. Your note cards are out of order. You know the audience is waiting to tear you to shreds, and you can't remember the words to your introduction. "Why did I ever take this class?" you ask yourself. "I am terrified. Just listen to the roaring in my ears. I can't breathe. I'm going to faint!" STOP! WAKE UP! This is a nightmare — not Communication 100! Nervousness and apprehension are NORMAL before and during a public presentation. There are ways to make this extra energy work for you and not against you. Here are the most common forms of advice given by experts. Read them carefully and try them out.

1. Keep the physical responses in a reasonable, manageable range. Sleep and eat well before your speech. Take care of your health in general. As you prepare for your speech, do yoga, exercise, sing, or whatever helps you relax every time you feel your anxiety increasing. Right before your speech, do something physical: take a walk or a run. Take a deep breath before your speech. Relax your arms and facial muscles. Take a drink of water before you begin.

2. Keep your thoughts positive. As you prepare for the speech, visualize yourself speaking in a confident manner. Contradict negative thoughts with positive ones. For example, "I have nothing interesting to say" can be eliminated with, "I have done enough research to make this an interesting presentation." Before the speech, label your physical sensations positively as "psyched-up excitement," rather than "paralytic fear."

3. Keep your focus on your audience and your message, not on yourself. Your audience members want you to succeed. They are very sympathetic and appreciative of your feelings. They are not the "enemy."

4. Pick a topic that interests you, and let your enthusiasm show. Make scrupulous preparations through research, a clear outline, and lots of evidence. Practice adequately. Practice with real people, and practice in the room if possible. Have a strong introduction and know it well.

5. Act as though you are confident, even if you are not. Your audience seldom perceives you to be as nervous as you know you are, so bluff a little. Here are some clear behaviors you can adopt that project confidence:
   - Walk confidently to the podium — arrange your notes and visual aids exactly how you want them
   - Place your feet squarely on the floor before you begin
   - Establish eye contact with the audience and pause before starting
   - Speak slowly and clearly
   - Use gestures that feel natural
   - Do not memorize your speech
   - If you make a blunder, just pause and regain your composure. Don't draw attention to the fact that you messed up by screwing up your face, laughing, or saying you forgot!

PERSONAL REPORT OF PUBLIC SPEAKING ANXIETY
(PRPSA)

Instructions:

This instrument is composed of thirty-four statements concerning feelings about communicating with other people. Work quickly; just record your first impression. Indicate the degree to which the statements apply to you by marking whether you

(1)	(2)	(3)	(4)	(5)
Strongly Agree	Agree	Are Undecided	Disagree	Strongly Disagree

_____ 1. While preparing for giving a speech, I feel tense and nervous.

_____ 2. I feel tense when I see the words "speech" and "public speech" on a course outline.

_____ 3. My thoughts become confused and jumbled when I am giving a speech.

_____ 4. Right after giving a speech, I feel that I have had a pleasant experience.

_____ 5. I get anxious when I think about a speech coming up.

_____ 6. I have no fear of giving a speech.

_____ 7. Although I am nervous just before starting a speech, I soon settle down after starting and feel calm and comfortable.

_____ 8. I look forward to giving a speech.

_____ 9. When the instructor announces a speaking assignment in class, I can feel myself getting tense.

_____ 10. My hands tremble when I am giving a speech.

_____ 11. I feel relaxed while giving a speech.

_____ 12. I enjoy preparing for a speech.

_____ 13. I am in constant fear of forgetting what I prepared to say.

_____ 14. I get anxious if someone asks me something about my topic that I do not know.

_____ 15. I face the prospect of giving a speech with confidence.

_____ 16. I feel that I am in complete possession of myself while giving a speech.

_____ 17. My mind is clear when giving a speech.

_____ 18. I do not dread giving a speech.

_____ 19. I perspire just before starting a speech.

_____ 20. My heart beats very fast just as I start a speech.

_____ 21. I experience considerable anxiety while sitting in the room just before my speech starts.

_____ 22. Certain parts of my body feel very tense and rigid while giving a speech.

_____ 23. Realizing that only a little time remains in a speech makes me very tense and anxious.

_____ 24. While giving a speech I can control my feelings of tension and stress.

_____ 25. I breath faster just before starting a speech.

_____ 26. I feel comfortable and relaxed in the hour or so just before giving a speech.

_____ 27. I do poorer on speeches because I am anxious.

_____ 28. I feel anxious when the teacher announces the date of a speaking assignment.

_____ 29. When I make a mistake while giving a speech, I find it hard to concentrate on the parts that follow.

_____ 30. During an important speech, I experience a feeling of helplessness building up inside of me.

_____ 31. I have trouble falling asleep the night before a speech.

_____ 32. My heart beats very fast while I present a speech.

_____ 33. I feel anxious while waiting to give my speech.

_____ 34. While giving a speech, I get so nervous, I forget facts I really know.

To determine your score on the PRPSA, complete the following steps:

1. Add the scores for items 1, 2, 3, 5, 9, 10, 13, 14, 19, 20, 21, 22, 23, 25, 27, 28, 29, 30, 31, 32, 33 and 34.

2. Add the scores for items 4, 6, 7, 8, 11, 12, 15, 16, 17, 18, 24, and 26.

3. Complete the following formula:
   PRPSA = 132 − (total from step one) + (total from step two).

Your score should range between 34 and 170. If your score is below 34 or above 170, you have made a mistake in computing the score.

Scores Between	Indicate
34 and 84	Low anxiety about public speaking (5%)
85 and 92	Moderately low level of anxiety about public speaking (5%)
93 and 110	Moderate anxiety in most public speaking situations (20%)
111 and 119	Moderately high level of anxiety about public speaking (30%)
120 and 170	Very high level of anxiety about public speaking (40%)

* MOST people score in the moderate to high categories!
Note: Complete one of these forms at the beginning of the semester and one after your final speech. Compare your total scores, as well as your responses to individual items.

Source: Richmond, P. V. & McCroskey, J. C. (1985). *Communication Apprehension, Avoidance, and Effectiveness.* Scottsdale, AZ: Gorsuch Scarisbrick.

Speech Outline

Title: laser eye surgery: To do or not to do.

Speaker: Ian Stewart—George Mason University student

Specific Purpose: To inform the audience of the risks and rewards of laser eye surgery.

Thesis Statement: Laser eye surgery may seem like a miracle cure to those who need corrective glasses or contacts, but in some cases, it does not live up to the perfect eyesight challenge.

Introduction

I.   Attention-getter: You are watching your favorite NFL team (Redskins or Cowboys?) or going to see Moby or Faith Hill in concert for the first time, and you realize that you forgot your glasses! Your contacts are rolling behind your eye! Things are just not as clear as they once were. You say you see clearly now but, in time, age will likely take its toll on your 20/20 vision and you may end up like, well, Mr. Magoo?

II. Establishment of Ethos: That is why I am here to tell you about laser eye surgery. I have some friends and acquaintances who think it is a miracle. I'm thinking about having laser eye surgery and certainly want to know what I might be getting into!

III. Thematic Statement: Laser eye surgery may seem like a miracle cure to those who need corrective glasses or contacts, but in some cases, it does not live up to the perfect eyesight challenge.

IV. Preview (each main point): I will explain why some tend to see better than others. Then, I will talk about two of the types of laser eye surgery, followed by some of the potential risks involved.

(Transition-Now, why can't all people see perfectly?)

Body

I.   Main Idea #1: Alvin and Virginia Silverstein (1989) indicate several reasons why some people have problems seeing things either at a distance or close-up. The authors define myopia, hyperopia, and presbyopia.

   A.   Sub-point and/or Supporting Material: Myopia, or nearsightedness, is where you can see things clearly when they are close to you, but have difficulty focusing on things far away. The causation is that the lens and cornea of the eye bend the light too much, the image falls short of the retina.

   B.   Sub-point and/or Supporting Material: For hyperopia, or farsightedness, the light rays are not bent enough, and so the image lands behind the retina. This will often make objects that are close seem blurry.

   C.   For those of you who currently see perfectly, there is something that even you cannot escape, that is presbyopia. Silverstein and Silverstein (1989) point out that the onset of presbyopia makes it difficult for those over 40 years of age to focus on close objects.

D. The human eye does not reach its final size and shape until about the age of 18. So, if you have seen well up to now, you are likely to continue to see well (since most of you are around 18 years old), but it's all downhill from here!

(Internal Summary: So, the most common visibility problems we have are myopia — where you can see things closely, but things at a distance become blurry; hyperopia — where things that are close seem blurry, and, presbyopia, which impacts most older adults' ability to focus on close objects.)

(Transition: Okay, you know why you have or will have problems seeing. Now, how does laser eye surgery help?)

II. Main Idea #2: In laser eye surgery, there are two different refractive procedures, which vary slightly in procedure and have different possible side effects (Muller, 1999). The first is photo refractive keratectomy, or PRK for short. The second is laser in-situ keratomileusis, or LASIK.

A. Sub-point and/or supporting Material: With PRK, no cutting is done. Instead, a computer-driven excimer laser uses a cool beam of light to sculpt or reshape the cornea so that images fall directly onto the retina. With myopia, the cornea is flattened; in cases of hyperopia or presbyopia, the cornea is reshaped so that it is steeper than before.

B. Sub-point and/or Supporting Material: In LASIK, a flap of cornea tissue is surgically cut. The flap is put back on the cornea to bond again with the eye.

C. So, what are the differences? Well, first, the FDA has approved only PRK, while LASIK is still undergoing the approval process. Jacqueline Muller (1999), a surgeon who has performed many eye corrections, claims that "most PRK patients gain functional vision within one to three days, and most LASIK patients have functional vision within 12 hours" (p. 12).

(Internal Summary: To reiterate, strong differences in the two procedures for laser eye correction are as follows: With PRK, a computer-driven laser removes parts of the cornea, as opposed to LASIK, where a surgeon first cuts a flap of the eye then a laser removes area from the underside of the flap. LASIK has a quicker recovery time of roughly 12 hours, whereas PRK may take one to three days. As of now, PRK is FDA approved; LASIK is not FDA approved.)

(Transition: You have heard all the good that laser eye surgery can do, but what are the risks involved?)

III. Main Idea #3: As with any new cutting-edge process, there are certain drawbacks to laser eye surgery. As Ralph Rosenthal stated in the *FDA Consumer Magazine* "some can end up with worse eyesight than before they went in" (Lewis, 1999, p. 22). Thus, with surgery there are risks involved.

A. Sub-point and/or Supporting Material: 63% of patients experienced some cornea haze (Snider, 1995).

B. Sub-point and/or Supporting Material: 10% experienced glare and halos around lights (Snider, 1995), but this eventually went away.

C. Sub-point and/or Supporting Material: With LASIK, the eye flap could be damaged.

D. Of course, there could also be over- or under-correction.

(Internal Summary/Transition to Conclusion: So there can be a downside to laser eye surgery, but, then again, nothing can be gained without risk.)

Conclusion

I. Summarize (overall theme): Laser eye surgery has given those people with imperfect vision a chance to go without the hassle of contacts and glasses.

II. Review (each main point): I have gone over the basic reasons why some people tend to see better than others. I have informed you of the latest technological advances for improving eyesight, including PRK and LASIK approaches, as well as the problems that may occur.

III. Tie to the introduction/creative concluding thought (end with impact): So, the next time you are about to head out the door to your favorite sightseeing event and you are having trouble tracking down your glasses or lose a contact, remember that you do have options. You can either improve your memory, or your eyes!

References

Lewis, C. (1999). Laser eye surgery: Is it worth looking into? *FDA Consumer Magazine.*

Muller, J. W. (1999). *Refractive errors.* Retrieved on March 01, 2000 from, http://www.laser-eyesurgery.com/errors.html.

Sekuler, R. (1982). *Aging and human visual function (Ed.).* New York, NY: Alan R. Liss Inc. Silverstein, A., & Silverstein, V. (1989). Glasses and contact lenses. New York, NY: J. B. Lippincott.

Snider, S. (1995). FDA expected to approve eye laser for nearsightedness. Retrieved on March 01, 2000 from, www.fad.gov/bbs/topics/ANSWERS/ANS00682.html.

Dixon, J. A., & Foster, D. H. (1998). Gender, social context, and backchannel responses. *The Journal of Social Psychology, 138*(1), 134-136.

Annotated Bibliography

Using a sample of 104 English-speaking, South African Undergraduates (50 men and 54 women), the authors examine gender differences in backchanneling — defined as listeners' use of verbal and nonverbal signals to display attentiveness to speakers. The study consisted of groups of 2 speakers, one male and one female, engaging in either a competitive or noncompetitive dialogue in which they were either told to get to know each other or assigned a topic for debate. Each conversation lasted about 8 minutes.

The authors found that there was no significant main effect of speaker gender for either nonverbal or verbal backchanneling. However, backchanneling was less frequent for competitive dialogue. They also found that men use more support signals than women when addressing a female audience, contradicting the stereotype that men are unsupportive speakers.

No indication of age, appearance, or social status was given in this article. These factors may also play into the responsiveness of genders to each other. Additionally, topic of discussion may also have an influence on backchanneling behaviors, as well as duration of the conversation.

Appendix C

Review of Literature

Running head: CULTURE AND COMMUNICATION IN SDWTS

Does Cultural Diversity Affect Communication Effectiveness

in Self-Directed Work Teams?

Exceptional Student

University of Anyplace

Does Cultural Diversity Affect Communication Effectiveness
in Self-Directed Work Teams?

Just about every species on the planet uses teamwork at some point to ensure that it thrives and survives. It seems natural that organizations competing in the present survival-of-the-fittest economic environment seek to adopt a team structure, as well. To this end, academics have researched various models for team work since the early 1900s that allow organizations to provide more autonomy to employees, while producing an overall working environment that is conducive to higher productivity and product/service output (Balkema & Molleman, 1999).

Several models for organizational decision-making processes incorporating team work have been commonly employed, including quality circles, sociotechnical systems, quality of work life programs, gainsharing programs, employee stock option plans, and self-directed work teams, to name a few. Self-directed work teams, henceforth referred to as SDWTs, have gained much focus in academic research and among organizations in globally competitive markets for their believed flexibility and responsiveness to market pressures (Iles & Hayers, 1997). Research shows that 1 in 5 companies has or will soon implement self-directed work teams (Tudor, Trumble, & Diaz, 1996). Consequently, it is vital for organizations to understand the complicated processes that dictate the success of SDWTs, especially related to the levels of cultural diversity within these groups.

This review of literature highlights studies on the effects of cultural differences in creating and maintaining successful SDWTs. It will provide insight into: 1) cultural variations 2) the cultural impacts on SDWTs; and 3) the constructs for successful, culturally diverse SDWTs.

What is a Self-Directed Work Team?

Self-Directed Work Teams (SDWTs) were first developed by Eric Trist and his colleagues in the UK four decades ago (Attaran & Nguyen, 2000). In the United States, SDWTs have been implemented in various organization types since the 1960s. Stemming from other group models popular at that time, such as quality circles and sociotechnical systems, SDWTs were intended to promote employees' empowerment and encourage workers' participation as a means to enhance organizational performance; especially focused on improved quality, increased productivity, and decreased operating costs (Attaran & Nguyen, 2000; Rafferty & Tapsell, 2001). Researchers have found substantial benefits from the introduction of SDWTs in the workplace, for example, greater level of team productivity, improved quality, improved customer satisfaction, and greater safety (Rafferty & Tapsell, 2001).

As a result of both global competition and company downsizing, multinational companies are increasingly employing SDWTs in their foreign affiliates (Kirkman & Shapiro, 1997). Teams have been promoted in Europe for more than 30 years because of their beneficial effects on organizational effectiveness and the quality of working life (Van Amelsvoort & Benders, 1996). While these programs have proven successful in the United States, Japan, and many European countries (Attaran & Nguyen, 2000), restraints due to cultural differences, among other things, have hindered implementation of cross-cultural SDWTs (Alvarez-Robinson, 2000; Nicholls, Lane, & Brechu, 1999; Cotton, McFarlin, & Sweeney, 1993).

SDWTs are also commonly referred to as self-managed teams, self-organizing teams, self-maintaining teams, self-leading teams, semi-autonomous work groups, self-regulating groups, self-managed work groups, and many others in empirical research (Attaran & Nguyen, 2000). SDWTs are always composed of two essential components. The first component is the process of self-management — meaning groups of employees who are responsible for managing themselves. This usually includes assigning jobs to team members; planning and scheduling work; making production or service-related decisions, and taking action to remedy problems. The second component is teamwork — meaning the ability to work interdependently with other members of the team (Kirkman & Shapiro, 1997; Kirkman & Shapiro, 2001; Van Amelsvoort & Benders, 1996; Dreachslin, Hunt, & Sprainer, 2000; Ageeth & Molleman, 1999; Cohen & Bailey, 1997; Rafferty & Tapsell, 2001).

SDWTs have been implemented in various types of organizations, including, manufacturing, service, engineering, and others (Attaran & Nguyen, 2000; Dreachslin, Hunt, & Sprainer, 2000; Cotton, McFarlin, & Sweeney, 1993; Rafferty & Tapsel, 2001). They may vary in size from small groups of 5-15 employees to entire organizations working as a self-sustaining SDWT. Although past research suggested that size has a curvilinear or inverted U-shaped relationship to effectiveness of SDWTs, a more recent study by Cohen and Bailey (1997) found a positive relationship between group size and group productivity. Typically, the members of SDWTs are cross-trained in a variety of skills relevant to the tasks they perform (Cohen & Bailey, 1997), and rotate roles.

As the landscape of the workforce in the United States and abroad continues to evolve into a global environment, the lines distinguishing domestic and foreign have become blurred by trans-global relationships in business (Alvarez-Robinson, 2000). For this reason, organizations must recognize the valuable asset that culturally diverse SDWTs provide, and seek to employ methods to harness their full potential for economic growth. However, in order to understand growth potential, one must first understand what the term "culture" refers to.

Culture

Hofstede (1980) asserts that culture is dictated by an influence of deeply-rooted values or shared normative, moral, or aesthetic principles that guide action to serve as standards to evaluate one's own and other people's behavior. In order to provide an understanding of the distinctions between cultures, Hofstede (1980) developed his theory of four fundamental cultural dimensions — later adding a fifth — to identify and validate national cultural differences. His theory has been employed by almost every major study conducted on the effects of cultural diversity in SDWTs in the last 20 years (Rafferty & Tapsell, 2001; Kirkman & Shapiro, 1997; Kirkman & Shapiro, 2001; Iles & Hayers, 1997; Van Amelsvoort & Benders, 1996; Cohen & Bailey, 1997).

According to an updated version of Hofstede's theory (International Business Etiquette, n.d.), there are five independent dimensions of national cultural differences: power distance; individualism; masculinity; uncertainty avoidance, and long-term orientation. *Power distance* focuses on the degree of equality or inequality between people within a particular country's society. A high power distance indicates a large gap in inequalities of power and wealth, characteristic of a caste system that does not allow upward mobility of its citizens. A low power distance indicates minimal emphasis in the differences between a citizen's power and wealth, characteristic of societies where equality and opportunity for everyone is stressed. *Individualism* focuses on a society's emphasis on individualistic and collectivistic characteristics in terms of accomplishments and interpersonal relationships. High individualism indicates individuality and individual rights are paramount in the society, and low individualism indicates a society with a more collectivist nature — focused on group accomplishments. *Masculinity* focuses on the degree to which a society reinforces a traditional masculine work role model of male achievement, control, and power. High masculinity indicates a high degree of inequality among genders, with females falling into a role of subordination. In low-masculinity cultures, males and females are treated equally in all aspects of society. *Uncertainty Avoidance Index* indicates the level of tolerance for the unknown within a society. High uncertainty avoidance indicates a low tolerance for the unknown and varying opinions. These types of societies are very rules-oriented, and institute many laws to avoid uncertainty. Low uncertainty avoidance indicates a more risk-taking society that is less concerned with ambiguity and more open to alternative views, is less rules-oriented, and readily accepts change. The fifth dimension, *Long-term orientation,* was added by Hofstede after additional research (International Business Etiquette, n.d.). It focuses on the degree that a society embraces, or does not embrace long-term devotion to traditional, forward-thinking values. High long-term orientation indicates that the society values long-term commitments and respect for traditions. Business may take longer to develop in these societies. Low long-term orientation indicates a view of preferred rapid change.

In order to determine a culture's outlook, or factors determining interaction, each of the five variables is ranked and compared in relation to each other. These five variables can also be used to determine an appropriate course of action in business relationships with members from varying cultures. For instance, Mexican culture, which exhibits a very high power distance, very low individualism, very high masculinity, and very high uncertainty avoidance, values collectivism and authority, and is a male-dominated society with a large gap between the "haves" and the "have nots." In implementing SDWTs in Mexico or with Mexican workers, this model indicates that there may be great barriers to overcome in terms of gender equality, ability to function as an autonomous group, and ability to make decisions without the guidance of an authoritative figure. This is further supported by Nicholls, Lane, and Brehm's (1999) study of SDWTs in Mexican organizations, where they found great resistance to self-managed teams.

Researchers have used these five variables, along with many other variables to try to determine preferred work environments conducive to culturally diverse SDWTs. One very common distinction made between cultures in an attempt to explain certain behaviors is whether or not they are individualistic or collectivistic. In collectivistic cultures, the self is defined in relation to in-group memberships in which shared values and norms, common goals, and utilitarian relationships are highly regarded. In an individualistic culture, the self is defined in terms of autonomy, personal liberty, and the supremacy of self-interests over those of the group (Stephan, Saito, & Barnett, 1998; Sosik & Jung, 2002). Sosik and Jung elaborate further on the concepts of individualism and collectivism by explaining that group input (e.g., cultural context) variables influence patterns of group composition (e.g., functional heterogeneity, preference for teamwork) and progress (e.g., group potency, outcome expectation), and may affect group outcomes (e.g., performance) directly or through interactions.

Researchers have not obtained conclusive evidence to support either one of these variables as being more or less conducive to culturally diverse SDWTs. Sosik and Jung claim that members of collectivist cultures may not perform well in diverse work teams due to the emphasis on shared values, similarities, and commonness among group members, whereas individualists highlight differences among group members. Individualists view group diversity as a way to provide unique qualities and multiple perspectives on problem-solving. The authors found that contrary to previous studies, higher levels of "functional heterogeneity" and group effectiveness associated with individualistic groups may have encouraged group members to learn from each other, to focus on task rather than on social and interpersonal relations, and to build the confidence required for superior performance, whereas, collectivistic groups may have initially focused more effort on building social and interpersonal relations among their members. Thus, it may take much longer to see performance results and the resulting outcomes may be hindered by group-think. However, it remains unclear which cultural ideal, if any, provides a more favorable environment for the development of work groups (Sasik & Jung, 2002). Although, researchers contend that focusing on a culture's tendency toward collectivism or individualism, and also employing Hofstede's five variables in composing SDWTs can provide the means to produce successful teams (Kirkman & Shapiro, 1997; Kirkman & Shapiro, 2001).

Cultural Impacts on Self-Directed Work Teams

Of all types of work teams, SDWTs are the most effective in promoting diversity (Hayes, 1995). Robinson Hickman and Creighton-Zollar (1998) contend, "SDWTs may provide one of the most natural means for incorporating and promoting diversity in twenty-first century organizations (p.56)." However, in the last ten years, several studies conducted to determine the effects of cultural diversity on SDWTs have shown varying degrees of results, especially in terms of agreement about the benefits of these groups (Dreachslin, Hunt, & Sprainer, 2000; Cotton, McFarlin, & Sweeney, 1993; Sosik & Jung, 2002; Iles, Hayers, & Kaur, 1997; Nicholls, Lane, & Brechu, 1999; Cohen & Bailey, 1997; Robinson Hickman & Creighton-Zollar, 1998; Woodard, 1995; Rafferty & Tapsell, 2001; Kirkman & Shapiro, 2001).

SDWTs are often seen by managers as "quick fix" solutions for higher production rates, when in actuality, successful SDWTs take years of training and implementation processes (Van Amelsvoort & Benders, 1996). Several factors can inhibit an SDWT's success, such as, resistance to self-management, increased training costs, language and cognitive perception barriers, and time constraints. Successful SDWTs usually occur over the long-term, and the fluidity of cultures and group members over time (Cotton, McFarlin, & Sweeney, 1993; Kirkman & Shapiro, 2001; Robinson Hickman & Creighton-Zollar, 1998; Tudor, Trumble, & Diaz, 1996; Cohen & Bailey, 1996; Rafferty & Tapsell, 2001).

According to Dreachslin, Hunt and Sprainer, (2000), "theory and organizational research support the conclusion that organizational diversity has the potential to result in both positive and negative outcomes (p. 1408)." Many researchers are interested in understanding which factors result in positive outcomes when combined.

Cohen and Bailey (1997), in a comprehensive review of literature on team effectiveness research, conclude that evidence supports the following with respect to SDWTs: substantive participation in decision-making improves team outcomes; cohesive teams are better performers; team autonomy results in higher performance, and teams that collaborate and resolve conflicts increase member satisfaction. High achievement for these four indicators will be much more challenging for culturally diverse teams, than for culturally homogenous teams. However, current research has made some headway in determining variables that are necessary for successful, culturally diverse SDWTs. Through examination of cultural relationships in both domestic and foreign SDWTs, and comparison of findings to cross-national SDWTs, researchers have begun developing a loose framework for successful SDWTs in culturally diverse and globalized organizations. The underlying variables that determine the success or failure of culturally diverse SDWTs is training and effective communication. Other factors, such as collectiveness and individualism, play a role in SDWT success, but any hindrance to team success may be overcome with training and effective communication. Extensive training in areas determined by levels of culturally decided factors, such as self-efficacy, resistance to self-management, communication skills, etc., is what determines whether an SDWT succeeds or fails (Tudor, Trumble, & Diaz, 1996).

Constructs for Successful, Culturally Diverse SDWTs

With organizations increasingly relying on virtual teams and other long-distance collaborative work structures, findings suggest that managers in multinational organizations should pay attention to how group characteristics vary across cultures, especially how such variables may improve group performance (Sosik & Jung, 2002).

Watson and Kumar (1992) conclude although culturally diverse groups have the potential to generate a greater variety of ideas and other resources than culturally homogenous groups, they need to overcome some of the group interaction problems that make group functioning more difficult. To be effective, any work group needs to perceive, interpret and evaluate situations in ways that are comprehensible to all members and then agree on best decision (p. 61).

Maznevski (1994) observes the common element in high-performing groups with high member diversity is integration of that diversity. In all of these studies, diversity led to higher performance only when members were able to understand each other, combine, and build on each other's ideas (p. 537).

To this end, communication is an integral factor in successful culturally diverse SDWTs. "Effective communication serves as the integrative mechanism in diverse groups" (Maznezski, 1994, p. 546). However, language barriers often make effective communication difficult to achieve. Every culture places different meanings on certain words and actions. For instance, Indonesian culture considers it impolite to tell someone "no," so their language has twelve variations of the word "yes," each with different degrees of agreeability (International Business Etiquette, n.d.). To an outsider, it could be very confusing if you thought an Indonesian person was saying yes to all of your requests, when in actuality they might be saying "definitely," "maybe," "maybe not," or "absolutely not," based on the degree of the implied meaning in their yes answer. Language barriers coupled with varying cultural perceptions can lead to disasters in SDWTs without productive means to create understanding.

Kirkman & Shapiro, 1997 found that cross-cultural miscommunication frequently results from subconscious cultural blinders, which is the lack of conscious attention to cultural assumptions; the lack of cultural self-awareness, which is the ignorance associated with not knowing one's own cultural conditioning; and projected similarity, meaning the belief that people are more similar to one's self than they actually are.

Additionally, a culture's context, or the amount of information that a person can comfortably manage, may have an effect on effective communication within an SDWT. Cultures with a high context, such as the United States, are often well informed on many subjects, due to wider networks and the tendency to send more information implicitly, whereas members of cultures with a low context tend not to be well informed on subjects outside the realm of their interest. Many Latin American cultures are low in context. Context can create tension within a culturally diverse SDWT, with "know-it-all" types taking over the group decision-making processes and excluding lower-context members.

Another variable to consider in creating successful, culturally diverse SDWTs is time. Although collectivist cultures have many difficulties with change, Sosik and Jung (2002) observed that once collectivist cultures were working in SDWTs, they viewed group interaction as an opportunity to develop fulfilling relationships over time. Individualists, on the other hand, had a strong preference for short-term SDWTs that allowed them to rapidly accomplish goals and then move on. Thus, stronger preferences for teamwork may emerge for collectivists in the long-term.

Additionally, Van Amelsvoort and Benders (1996), found that gradual implementation of SDWTs allows team members an opportunity to become accustomed to their new roles over time, rather than all at once, thus reducing anxiety about their new autonomy and allowing for the building up of confidence in their capability to handle their new work situation. This may create a more positive long-term effect on the success of SDWTs.

Some other important variables in creating successful, culturally diverse SDWTs include fairness, trust, pay considerations and other rewards, and extensive employee training, (Hayes, 1995; Tudor, Trumble, & Diaz, 1996). Cultural constraints can impair SDWT members' abilities to interrelate all of the previously mentioned variables. However, if each team member can have at least a basic to intermediate understanding of the cultural motivations that sometimes drive decision-making processes, it might help in overcoming cultural barriers to working collectively to accomplish goals.

Conclusion

Although there is a substantive body of research on cultural effects on SDWTs, the recommendations of these studies vary on how to implement successful, culturally diverse SDWTs. Nearly every study of SDWTs has focused on their impact on effectiveness (Cohen & Bailey, 1997), not on how to shape the teams to achieve success (Roy, 2001). Broader studies concerning appropriate measures for developing successful SDWTs need to be researched in order to fully understand the outcomes of the current SDWT research. Understanding results does not help to remedy problems or replicate successes if organizations do not know why the results occurred. Additionally, proven ways to leverage the full potential of multi-cultural teams have not been clearly identified. There is considerable research on how culture can affect teams, but not on how cultural diversity can be utilized to enhance and promote successful group initiatives.

A distinction between cultural and institutional differences also needs to be established more clearly in research. For instance, Van Amelsvoort and Benders (1996) state, "cultural differences concern value systems, where institutional differences concern national institutions that exist in a national economy" (p. 161), that is, what the collective culture would like to see occur, as opposed to what societal constraints force to occur. This factor may make a difference in research results when individuals are taken out of their institutional or societal context.

Additionally, some researchers have argued that the distinction between individualism and collectivism masks many differences existing within each category; for example, Costa Rica and Japan are both collectivistic cultures, yet they bear little resemblance to each other (Stephan, Saito, & Morrisom Barnett, 1998). In this comparison, Hofstede's five cultural variables would be helpful in further distinguishing cultural differences.

Other variables that may hinder the development of a workable framework for an appropriate method for implementing culturally diverse SDWTs are language and conflict resolution. Word meaning within different cultures has the potential to skew results. For example, Benders, Huijgen, & Pekruhl (2002) illustrate in their analysis of studies on work groups that the word "team" has different meanings for different cultures, and can create potential for unequivocal comparisons of nationalities in work group environments. Japanese-inspired teams, for instance, contain a hierarchical structure, whereas "groups" holds the Anglo-Saxon meaning of the term "team," which infers autonomous participation. Thus, researching the presence and characteristics of "teams" in certain countries entails the risk of retaining answers based on completely different understandings of what "teams" are (Benders, Huijgen, & Pekruhl, 2002; Van Amelsvoort, & Benders, 1996).

A study by Alper, Tjosvold, and Law (2000) indicates that conflict can benefit groups and organizations as long as the groups have high conflict efficacy — confidence in team ability to cooperatively manage conflict in a productive manner. However, cultural differences may dictate how team members manage conflict. For instance, most collectivist cultures are conditioned to avoid conflict at all costs, therefore limiting the development of conflict efficacy within those groups. In other individualistic societies, people may thrive on conflict as a driving force for creativity. Teams made up of these two opposing dynamics may exhibit an environment where collectivist members lose their voice because they do not speak up in an effort to avoid conflict. Lastly, some cultures simply ignore conflict, which can create tension among team members who may feel a need to discuss the issues at hand.

Specific changes need to occur in the structure, processes, and policies of the organization in order to provide an appropriate environment for diverse SDWTs. These changes require attention to continuing support from management and upper-level administrators within the organization, purposeful structuring of diverse teams, establishing links between organizational and team goals, implementing training and education programs to support diverse team development, allowing adequate time to become a functional team, and changing policies, procedures, and reward systems to support teamwork (Robinson Hickman, & Creighton-Zollar, 1998).

Finally, because cultures are dynamic, rather than static, it cannot be assumed that classifications based on decades-old data are valid today (Stephan, Saito, & Morrisom Barnett, 1998). Additionally, all behavior is context specific.

References

Alper, S., Tjosvold, D., & Law, K. S. (2000). Conflict management, efficacy, and performance in organizational teams. *Personnel Psychology, 53,* 625-642.

Alvarez-Robinson, S. M. (2000). Enhancing multi-cultural work teams. Retrieved July 22, 2003, from www.alvarez-robinson.com.

Balkema, A., & Molleman, E., (1999). Barriers to the development of self-organizing teams. *Journal of Managerial Psychology, 14,* 134-149.

Benders, J., Huijgen, F., & Pekruhl, U. (2002). What do we know about the incidence of group work (if anything)? *Personnel Review, 31,* 371-385.

Cohen, S. G., Bailey, D. E., (1997). What makes teams work: Group effectiveness research from the shop floor to the executive suite. *Journal of Management, 23,* 239-290.

Cotton, J. L., McFarlin, D. B., & Sweeney, P. D. (1993). A cross-national comparison of employee participation. *Journal of Managerial Psychology, 8,* 10-26.

Dohse, K., Juergens, U., & Malsch, T. (1985). "From fordism' to toyotaism'?" The social organisation of the labour process in the Japanese automobile industry. *Politics and Society, 14*(2), 64-92.

Dreachslin, J. L., Hunt, P. L., & Sprainer, E. (2000). Workforce diversity: Implications for the effectiveness of health care delivery teams. *Social Science & Medicine, 50,* 1403-1414.

Hanson, L. (1998). Society and self-managing teams, *International Journal of Social Economics, 25,* 72-89.

Hayes, C. (1995). The new spin on corporate work teams. *Black Enterprise, 25*(11), 229- 233.

Hofstede, G. (1980). Motivation, leadership and organization: Do American theories apply abroad? *Organizational Dynamics,* Summer, 42-63.

Iles, P., & Paromjit, K. H. (1997). Managing diversity in transnational project teams: A tentative model and case study. *Journal of Managerial Psychology, 12,* 95-117.

International Business Etiquette. (n.d.). Geert Hofstede Analysis. Retrieved July 23, 2003, from http://www.cyborlink.com/besite/hofstede.htm.

Kirkman, B. L., & Shapiro, D. L. (2001). The impact of cultural values on job satisfaction and organizational commitment in self-managing work teams: The mediating role of employee resistance. *Academy of Management Journal Mississippi State, 44*(3), 557-569.

Kirkman, B. L., & Shapiro, D. L. (1997). The impact of cultural values on employee resistance to teams: Toward a model of globalized self-managing work team effectiveness. *Academy of Management Journal Mississippi State, 22*(3), 730-757.

Maznevski, M. L., (1994). Understanding our differences: Performance in decision-making groups with diverse members. *Human Relations, 47,* 531-552.

Nicholls, C. E., Lane, H. W., & Brechu, M. B. (1999). Taking self-managed teams to Mexico. *The Academy of Management Executives, 13*(3), 15-25.

Rafferty, J., & Tapsell, J., (2001). Self-managed work teams and manufacturing strategies: Cultural influences in the search for team effectiveness and competitive advantage. *Human Factors and Ergonomics in Manufacturing, 11,* 19-34.

Robinson Hickman, G., & Creighton-Zollar, A. (1998). Diverse self-directed work teams: Developing strategic initiatives for 21st century organizations. *Public Personnel Management, 27,* 187-200.

Roy, M. H. (2001). Small group communication and performance: Do cognitive flexibility and context matter? *Management Decision, 39*(4), 323-330.

Sosik, J. J., & Jung, D. I. (2002). Work-group characteristics and performance in collectivist and individualistic cultures. *The Journal of Social Psychology, 142,* 5-24.

Stephan, C. W., Saito, I., & Morrison Barnet, S. (1998). Emotional expression in Japanese and the United States: The monolithic nature of individualism and collectivism. *Journal of Cross Cultural Psychology, 29,* 728-749.

Tudor, T. R., Trumble, R. R., & Diaz, J. J. (1996). Work teams: Why do they often fail? *Society for Advancement of Management Journal, 61*(4), 31-40.

Van Amelsvoort, P., Benders, J. (1996). Team time: A model for developing self-directed work teams. *International Journal of Operations and Production, 16,* 159-171.

Woodard, W. M. (1995). Understanding Business Protocol. *Black Enterprise, 25*(9), 36-37.

Appendix D

Research Prospectus

Running head: ETHNOCENTRISM AND INTERETHNIC COMMUNICATION

The Role of Ethnocentrism in Initial Interethnic Communication: Do Stereotypes

Contribute to Uncertainty and Anxiety?

Jeannie McPherson

George Mason University

Abstract

According to Hecht, Ribeau, and Alberts (1989) "it appears that of the many factors which influence communication effectiveness, none may do so more than ethnic culture" (p. 387). In an effort to reveal how/if ethnocentrism and stereotypes affect people's uncertainty and anxiety in interethnic communication with a stranger, 200 undergraduate students participated in an experiment intended to test their ethnocentrism, their willingness to interact with strangers based on their ethnicity/race, and how their perceptions of ethnicities have been formed. The author employs vignettes to glean data regarding an individual's willingness to interact with strangers based on their ethnicity/race. Based on the data, the author will provide insight into how individuals form perceptions of other ethnic/racial groups, and will offer suggestions and strategies to reduce uncertainty and anxiety in initial interethnic communication.

The Role of Ethnocentrism in Initial Interethnic Communication:
Do Stereotypes Contribute to Uncertainty and Anxiety?

The United States is one of the most ethnically diverse countries (Toale & McCroskey, 2001). Historically, the political ideology of the U.S. has been based on a "melting pot" metaphor (Taylor & Porter, 1994), imagery intended to represent the blending, or assimilation, into the dominant American culture of the wide diversity of ethnic groups that have immigrated to the country. However, researchers have recently found that many members of ethnic minorities desire to maintain their distinct cultural heritage, rather than to assimilate into the "melting pot," or dominant white culture of the U.S. Hence, researchers have begun using the metaphor of a "tossed salad" (Lustig & Koester, 1999) to better represent the many different ethnic groups in the U.S., with distinct characteristics, dialects, and cultural practices that must be mixed to accomplish larger goals.

The desire of ethnic groups to maintain their distinctiveness, partnered with the U.S. Census Bureau's (2004) projection that the populations of ethnic minorities in America will rise over the next 50 years, while the white population will drastically fall, indicates a great need for scholars to examine interethnic communication to help members of these distinct groups understand each others' perspectives and enable them to better function together in society. Even in relatively small communities throughout the U.S., people interact with others from different ethnic groups on a daily basis (Neuliep, Chaudoir & McCroskey, 2001). According to Hecht, Ribeau, and Alberts (1989) "it appears that of the many factors which influence communication effectiveness, none may do so more than ethnic culture" (p. 387). However, Toale and McCroskey (2001), as well as Gudykunst and Hammer (1988), found that research on interethnic communication between same-culture individuals is very lacking.

The term ethnicity in communication literature has historically been described according to participant race (Andsager & Mastin, 2003; Orbe & Warren, 2000; Konrad & Harris, 2002; Leonard & Locke, 1993; Popp, Crawford, Marsh, & Peele, 2003). In their experiments, these researchers perform comparative communication studies by categorizing subjects according to the biological characteristic of skin color. For example, Leonard and Locke (1993) attempt to discover how stereotypes inhibit effective interethnic communication by having "Black" and "White" college students choose 10 characteristics from a list of 66 communication traits that they felt best characterized the other group's communication behavior. Based on their findings, Leonard and Locke concluded that both "Black" and "White" students perceived interethnic communication as potentially threatening. While appearances, such as skin color, may be initial indicators of difference among strangers, there are other, deeper underlying social reasons that also need to be explored for why people from different ethnicities may feel threatened by each other (Gallois, 2003).

More recently, researchers have expanded the definition of ethnicity to also include identity and perceptions of others. Toale and McCroskey (2001) define ethnic identity as having a sense of belonging to, and having knowledge and shared experiences of, a particular group. This perception of belonging is what distinguishes the construct of ethnicity from the more biological term "race." Chen (2000) combines phenotypic characteristics and perceived identity to define ethnicity as being socially constructed by people who exclusively share cultural traits, ancestry, physical appearance, or a sense of social belonging or loyalty to a group.

While it is clear that strong arguments exist to represent people according to ethnic identity, for the purpose of this study, the author defines ethnicity according to the more traditional definition of skin color and physical attributes. Since this study will examine how ethnocentrism contributes to anxiety and uncertainty in initial interethnic communication with a stranger, the author believes that characteristics based on appearances, such as skin color and other physical traits, are more salient for discovering how respondents will react. This idea is supported by Khmelkov and Hallinan's (1999) study, which found that race is salient in interpersonal attraction, and Gudykunst (2004) who found that we tend to be attracted to strangers who appear similar to us. Specific races to be examined are African-American, Asian-American, Caucasian, Hispanic-American, and Middle Eastern.

Communication Styles/Stereotypes

According to Toale and McCroskey (2001) an individual's ability to effectively communicate in interethnic conversations with strangers is largely dependent on psychological factors, such as his or her level of ethnocentrism, and perceptions held about other ethnic groups. Moreover, unique communication behaviors are employed by members of different ethnic groups and may inhibit effective interethnic communication (Toale & McCroskey,

2001; Lapinski & Levine, 2000; Hecht, Ribeau, & Alberts, 1989; Leonard & Locke, 1993). In order to communicate effectively, one must have an understanding of an interactant's customs and perceptions (Gudykunst, 2004). Kirkman and Shapiro (1997) found that cross-cultural miscommunication often results from subconscious blinders, or the lack of attention to cultural assumptions, which frequently result in projected similarity — the belief that people are more similar to one's self then they actually are. The same can also apply to interethnic communication. For example, Hispanic-American people are often more comfortable than are European-American individuals when in close physical proximity to other people (Hall 1990). Without this knowledge, a European-American person interacting with a Hispanic-American person may take the closeness as an inappropriate advance, while the Hispanic-American person may see the European-American person's distance as rude. Further, scholars of Asian-American communication patterns have noted that there are important differences between Asian-Americans and European-Americans in their nonverbal expression styles (Uba, 1994). Asian-Americans tend to be more reserved in communicating their feelings, try to seek control over their emotions, avoid expressing strong feelings, and avoid direct eye contact, unlike European-Americans.

The above mentioned differences in communication style make it important to study such obstacles involved in interethnic communication to enable scholars and individuals to develop strategies for effective interethnic communication. Another obstacle discussed by Toale and McCroskey (2001), and a primary idea investigated in the current study, is that the knowledge of these style differences, compounded by common stereotypes, can elevate uncertainty and anxiety in interethnic communication. Leonard and Locke (1993) found that "White" participants believed "Black" people's speech to be loud, ostentatious, aggressive, active, boastful, talkative, noisy, straightforward, emotional, argumentative, and witty. These characteristics caused "White" participants to feel threatened by "Black" individuals. Popp, et al. (2003) found that "Black" Americans' speech is believed to be less socially appropriate and more direct than "White" Americans' speech. "Black" Americans' speech is also viewed as more emotional and less playful. Further, "Black" speakers were depicted as using more nonstandard speech forms, such as slang, profanity, and variant pronunciation and grammar than "White" speakers. Chen (2000) also notes that common stereotypes play a role in perception. Hence, Asia people are seen positively as intelligent, submissive, and wise, whereas recent events, such as the war in Iraq, have placed a negative stigma on people from Middle Eastern descent (Salari, 2002).

The idea is that all cultures are so imbedded in their own special codes and value orientations that there is an ethnocentric inclination to believe that their unique interpretations and perceptions of the world and human nature are the best and most correct ones (Neuliep, Chaudoir, & McCroskey, 2001). When faced with the possibility of interacting with people who are different from them, some people may experience elevated anxiety due to uncertainty about the behaviors and motivations that the unknown person will exhibit. Buss (1980) argues that some of the salient situational features leading to increased anxiety include novelty, unfamiliarity, and dissimilarity, such as ethnic/racial differences. This notion is explained through Berger and Calabrese's (1975) Uncertainty Reduction Theory, and Gudykunst's (1993), (1995), (2004) Anxiety/Uncertainty Management Theory.

Uncertainty Reduction Theory

Berger and Calabrese's (1975) Uncertainty Reduction Theory (URT) is grounded in the idea that the beginnings of personal relationships are fraught with uncertainties. The authors view the reduction of uncertainty as a central, mediating mechanism for explaining communication behavior. To reduce and overcome uncertainty, individuals use communication to gain knowledge and create understanding by making practical predictions about the other's attitudes, values, feelings, beliefs, and behavior, and by creating plausible explanations for the other's behavior based on previous experience. The desire to reduce uncertainty is driven by three factors: anticipation of future interaction; perceived benefits or gains; and explanation of deviant behavior (Berger, 1979). Seven axioms and 21 theorems were identified that specified the relationships among uncertainty, nonverbal affiliative expressiveness, amount of information, intimacy, information-seeking, reciprocity, and similarity and attraction in the URT's original formulation (Berger & Calabrese, 1975). This theory has been found to be very robust in human communication studies in the U.S. (Hammer, et al., 1998).

Anxiety/Uncertainty Management Theory

Anxiety/Uncertainty Management Theory (AUM) is based on the pioneering work of Berger and his associates (Berger, 1979, 1987; Berger & Bradac, 1982; Berger & Calabrese, 1975). Gudykunst and Hammer (1987) extended URT by incorporating anxiety reduction processes to explain intercultural adaptation, while Gudykunst (1988; 1993; 1995) extended URT to explain intergroup/interethnic interaction and communication effectiveness. This theoretical extension incorporates both cognitive (uncertainty reduction) and affective (anxiety reduction) dimensions and suggests that the dual processes of uncertainty reduction and anxiety reduction are key mediating variables for intercultural/interethnic adaptation (Hammer, et al., 1998).

Uncertainty refers to the inability to predict or explain the behavior of others (Neuliep & Ryan, 1998). As stated earlier, uncertainty reduction is a cognitive process in which the individual attempts to understand another's situation by making practical predictions about the other's attitudes, values, feelings, beliefs, and behaviors, and by creating plausible explanations for the other's behaviors, based on previous experiences. Gudykunst (1993) extends this notion by claiming that uncertainty is greater in interethnic/intercultural communication. According to Neuliep and Ryan, anxiety is a complex emotional response marked by subjective feelings or tension, apprehension, and worry regarding potentially negative outcomes. It manifests itself in feelings of discomfort, distress, and fear. There is a positive relationship between uncertainty and anxiety such that the more an individual is uncertain about a person or group, the more anxious he or she will be when faced with the potential for interacting with that person or group. Gudykunst (1995) argues that effective interethnic communication is based on the ability to manage anxiety and uncertainty.

The uncertainty experienced by individuals is often compounded by prevailing stereotypes in society. Harwood and Anderson (2002) found that depictions of ethnic groups on television can shape viewers' orientations to their own and other social groups, such that they tend to make demographic estimates that are closer to the television population than the actual population, and Mastro (2003) found that negatively stereotypical racial depictions in mediated messages were significantly associated with social judgments. This finding is particularly alarming since research also has shown that ethnic minority groups are often depicted negatively and inaccurately by the media (Harwood & Anderson, 2002).

Additionally, Kim (1990) identifies ingroup bias (i.e. ethnocentrism) as an obstacle to effective interethnic communication. Neuliep, Chaudoir and McCroskey (2001) believe that "a principal concept in understanding intergroup communication is ethnocentrism" (p. 135). Levinson (1950) argued that ethnocentrism is

> "based on a pervasive and rigid ingroup-outgroup distinction; it involves stereotyped, negative imagery and hostile attitudes regarding outgroups, stereotyped positive imagery and submissive attitudes regarding ingroups, and a hierarchical, authoritarian view of group interaction in which ingroups are rightly dominant, outgroups subordinate" (p. 150)

Several other scholars have argued that ethnocentrism is a universal phenomenon experienced to some degree in all cultures (Lewis, 1985; Lustig & Koester, 1999; Rushton, 1989). Gudykunst and Nishida (1994) maintain that everyone is ethnocentric to some degree and that, while it may be possible and preferable to have a low degree of ethnocentrism, to be nonethnocentric is impossible. Gudykunst and Kim (1997) contend that ethnocentrism is dysfunctional with respect to intercultural/interethnic relationships in that it influences the way people communicate with others. The consequences of an ethnocentric bias may be more serious in a diversely populated country, such as the United States, than in countries with homogenous populations, such as Japan (Neuliep, Chaudoir & McCroskey, 2001). Luestig and Koester (1999) believe competent intercultural interactants do not necessarily suppress ethnocentric attitudes, but instead recognize their existence and strive to minimize their impact on social interaction.

Drawing from Neuliep and McCroskey (1997) and Toale and McCroskey's (2001) work on ethnocentrism and Gudykunst (1989; 1993; 1995) and Gudykunst and Hammer's (1988) Anxiety/Uncertainty Management Theory, the author of this study will attempt to glean data on the how ethnocentrism and stereotypes shape individuals' perceptions about ethnic groups and how those perceptions affect uncertainty and anxiety in initial interethnic communication. Previous research (Toale & McCroskey, 2001) examined the extent to which ethnocentrism and trait communication apprehension are predictive of interethnic communication apprehension by asking participants to respond to Neulips and McCroskey's (1997) ethnocentrism scale and Neuliep and McCroskey's (1997) Personal Report of Interethnic Communication Apprehension (PRECA). The authors found a positive relation between ethnocentrism and interethnic communication apprehension. The author of this study expects to find a positive relationship between levels of ethnocentrism and levels of uncertainty and anxiety in interethnic communication based on Toale and McCroskey's (2001) findings and the assumption that communication apprehension and uncertainty and anxiety are related.

RQ$_1$: What is the role of ethnocentrism in initial interethnic communication?

RQ$_2$: How does ethnocentrism affect anxiety/uncertainty management?

RQ$_3$: How does prior experience with an ethnic group affect anxiety/uncertainty management?

Gudykunst (2004) says that in order for interethnic communication to occur, an individual must be motivated to communicate, and that motivation is driven by trust in an expected positive response. Based on Gudykunst's (2004) research, the author formulated the following hypotheses in regard to the research questions:

H1: The higher an individual's level of ethnocentrism is, the less likely he or she is to communicate with strangers from differing ethnic/racial backgrounds.

H2: Individuals are more likely to seek out members from his or her own ethnicity/race when there is a need to communicate with strangers.

H3: The more prior interaction an individual has had with a particular ethnicity/race, the more likely he or she will be to interact with other members from that particular ethnicity/race.

H3a: If a person's only knowledge of another ethnicity/race was developed from watching television, then their willingness to communicate with others from that ethnicity/race will depend on how that race was portrayed on television; i.e. African-Americans are commonly portrayed as criminals (Harwood & Anderson, 2002), thus a person from a different ethnicity/race will try to avoid interaction with African-Americans.

Method

The author will recruit no less than 200 participants (n=100) representing various ethnic/racial backgrounds from required college courses, such as English or Math, to respond to Neuliep's (2002) revised ethnocentrism scale (see Appendix A), which uses a 5-point Likert-type scale to measure 22 items intended to reveal an individual's level of ethnocentrism — an individual's belief that his/her unique interpretations and perceptions of the world and human nature are the best and most-correct ones. Of the 22 items, 15 are scored. The other seven are included to balance the number of positively and negatively worded items. Drawing from required courses will help avoid any bias that could occur by selecting participants from communications or cultural studies courses, for example, who may have a bias toward more effective intercultural/ethnic communication. The test will be anonymous, but will ask respondents to identify their ethnicity/race from the choices: African-American, Asian-American, Caucasian, Hispanic-American, Middle Eastern, and Other.

Immediately following the completion of the ethnocentrism scale, the participants will be instructed to respond to two vignettes developed by the author with guidance from Finch (1987), and Gudykunst and Hammer (1987) to depict situations for potential interethnic communication in which the participant has a desire that needs to be satisfied (see Appendix B). The vignettes were developed in this fashion to test whether or not a correlation exists between an individual's ethnocentrism and his or her willingness to communicate with people from other ethnic/racial backgrounds. An indicated need is inserted into each vignette as a motivational drive to instigate communication.

Since situational and contextual similarities can play a role in lessening or increasing uncertainty and anxiety (Albertson, 2001; Gudykunst, 2004), the author sought to remove these effects by depicting the characters in the vignette as people similar in age and dress to the respondent. No sex was identified, and the setting for each interaction is in a public, nonthreatening place; a park and a coffee shop. The vignettes are framed such that respondents will be asked to choose a response from a 5-point Likert-type scale, ranging from strongly disagree to strongly agree, according to how anxious or nervous they would be to approach the character to ask for the time or directions. The author distinguishes between ethnicity/race in the vignettes to reveal whether or not the degree of anxiety about interethnic communication varies according to the ethnicity of the character in the vignette. Dyadic communication situations were chosen for this study to eliminate any additional effect of apprehension or anxiety from the portrayed situations. Previous research (McCroskey, 1977; Toale & McCroskey, 2001; Gudykunst & Hammer, 1987) has shown that when individuals communicate with groups of strangers, their communication apprehension, or anxiety, is generally greater than when they communicate in dyadic situations.

Although not commonly used in communication research, the vignette technique was employed here primarily because vignettes provide concrete examples that define situations and, therefore, reduce ambiguity of responses. Findings from previous research (Toale & McCroskey, 2001) are limited, since conclusions were drawn from data collected when participants were instructed to recall previous interactions with another from a differing ethnic background. Basing conclusions on data collected according to a person's memory leaves much room for ambiguity and is a large limitation. Although vignettes may still suffer from the limitation of participants responding according to what they believe is the socially desirable answer (Finch, 1987), making the test anonymous should help alleviate this limitation and provide more concrete data. Moreover, vignettes are productive tools that offer a way to quantitatively measure participants' responses about issues that have the potential to provide discomfort in interviews and focus groups, such as ethnicity/race (Fitch, 1987). They have been used to elicit data about respondents' attitudes, beliefs, and ethical frameworks about a specific situation, and can easily be manipulated in testing for different variables (Finch, 1987). (See Gudykunst & Hammer, 1987; Miller, Boster, Roloff, & Seibold, 1977, for examples of communication research with vignettes, and Gerbert, Berg-Smith, Mancuso, Caspers, Danley, Herzig, & Brand, 2003; Adamson, Ben-Shlomo, Chaturvedi, & Donovan, 2003, for examples of research on health issues that employ vignettes based on ethnicity).

Finally, participants will be asked to respond to a set of questions intended to indicate how much experience they have with each ethnicity/race identified in this study and the source of their experience (see Appendix C). Participants will be asked to fill in blanks with a number ranging from 1 through 5, according to how how much they agree with the preceding statements. The same Likert-type measurements of strongly disagree to strongly agree will be assigned to the numbers. These questions are intended to determine where/how the participants' perceptions of the identified ethnic groups have been developed. The author will use the data collected from this section to test whether there is a correlation between prior experience with an ethnicity and a willingness to communicate with members from that ethnicity. Additionally, the author will test whether there is a correlation between prior experience with an ethnicity and levels of ethnocentrism. Each of the above-described testing procedures will take place at the same time. The full test should take no more than 20 minutes, and will be administered and collected by the author. It will be completed in a classroom environment at the beginning of class.

References

Adamson, J., Ben-Shlomo, B., Chaturvedi, N., & Donovan, J. (2003). Ethnicity, socio-economic position and gender — do they affect reported health-care seeking behaviour? *Social Science & Medicine*, 57(5), 895-904.

Andsager, J. L., & Mastin, T. (2003). Racial and regional differences in readers' evaluations of the credibility of political columnists by race and sex. *Journalism and Mass Communication Quarterly, 80,* 57-72.

Berger, C. R. (1979). Beyond initial interactions. In H. Giles & R. St. Clair (Eds.), *Language and social psychology*. Oxford: Basil Blackwell.

Berger, C. R. & Bradac, J. J. (1982). *Language and social knowledge: Uncertainty interpersonal relations*. London: Edward Arnold.

Berger, C. R. & Calabrese, R. (1975). Some explorations in initial interactions and beyond: Toward a developmental theory of interpersonal communication. *Human Communication Research, 1,* 99-112.

Buss, A. H. (1980). *Self-consciousness and social anxiety*. San Francisco, CA: W. H. Freeman & Company.

Chen, Z. (2000). Chinese American children's ethnic identity; Measurement and implications. *Communication Studies, 51,* 74-95.

Comer, L. B. & Nicholls, J. A. F. (2000). Communication between Hispanic salespeople and their customers: A first look. *Journal of Personal Selling & Sales Management, 20,* 121.

Finch, J. (1987). The vignette technique in survey research. *Sociology, 21,* 105-114.

Gallois, C. (2003). Reconciliation through communication in intercultural encounters: Potential or peril? *Journal of Communication, 53,* 5-15.

Gerbert, B., Berg-Smith, S., Mancuso, M., Caspers, N., Danley, D., Herzig, K., & Brand, R. (2003). Video study of physician selection: Preferences in the face of diversity. *Journal of Family Practice, 52*(7), 552-559.

Gudykunst, W. B. (2004). An Anxiety/Uncertainty Management (AUM) theory of effective communication: Making the mesh of the net finer. In W. B. Gudykunst (Ed.). *Theorizing about communication and culture*, Thousand Oaks, CA: Sage.

Gudykunst, W. B. (1995). Anxiety/uncertainty management (AUM) theory: Current status. In R. L. Wiseman (Eds.), *Intercultural communication theory* (pp. 8-58). Thousand Oaks, CA: Sage.

Gudykunst, W. B. (1993). Toward a theory of effective interpersonal and intergroup communication: An anxiety/uncertainty management (AUM) perspective. In R. L. Wiseman & J. Koester (Eds.), *Intercultural communication competence* (pp. 33-72). Newbury Park, CA: Sage.

Gudykunst, W. B. (1989). Culture and the development of interpersonal relationships. In J. A. Anderson (Ed.), *Communication yearbook 12* (pp. 315-354). Newbury Park, CA: Sage.

Gudykunst, W. B. & Hammer, M. R. (1988). The influence of social identity and intimacy of interethnic relationships on uncertainty reduction processes. *Human Communication Research, 14,* 569-601.

Gudykunst, W. B. & Hammer, M. R. (1987). The influence of ethnicity, gender, and dyadic composition on uncertainty reduction in initial interactions. *Journal of Black Studies, 18,* 191-214.

Gudykunst, W. B. & Kim, Y. Y. (1997). *Communicating with strangers: An approach to intercultural communication*. New York, NY: McGraw-Hill.

Gudykunst, W. B. & Nishida, T. (1994). *Bridging Japanese/North American differences*. Thousand Oaks, CA: Sage.

Hall, E. T. (1990). *The hidden dimension*. Garden City, New York, NY: Doubleday.

Hammer, M. R., Wiseman, R. L., Rasmussen, J. L., & Bruschke, J. C. (1998). A test of Anxiety/Uncertainty Management Theory: The intercultural adaptation context. *Communication Quarterly, 46,* 309.

Harwood, J. & Anderson, K. (2002). The presence and portrayal of social groups on prime-time television. *Communication Reports, 15,* 81-97.

Hecth, M. L., Ribeau, S., & Alberts, J. K. (1989). An Afro-American perspective on interethnic communication. *Communication Monographs, 56,* 385-410.

Khmelkov, V. T., & Hallinan, M. T. (1999). Organizational effects on race relations in schools. *Journal of Social Issues*, Winter, 42-58.

Kim, Y. Y. (1990, November). *Explaining interethnic conflict: An interdisciplinary overview*. Paper presented at the meeting of the Speech Communication Association, Chicago, IL.

Kirkman, B. L., & Shapiro, D. L. (1997). The impact of cultural values on employee resistance to teams: Toward a model of globalized self-managing work team effectiveness. *Academy of Management Review, 22*(3), 730-757.

Konrad, A. M., & Harris, C. (2002). Desirability of the Bem Sex-Role Inventory items for women and men: A comparison between African-Americans and European-Americans. *Sex Roles, 47,* (5/6), 259-271.

Leonard, R., & Locke, D. C. (1993). Communication Stereotypes: Is interracial communication possible? *Journal of Black Studies, 23,* 332-343.

Levinson, D. J. (1950). Politico-economic ideology and group memberships in relation to ethnocentrism. In T. W. Adorno, E. Frenkel-Brunswik, D. J. Levinson, & R. N. Sanford. *The authoritarian personality,* (pp. 151-221). New York: Harper & Brothers.

Lustig, M. W., & Koester, J. (1999). *Intercultural competence: Interpersonal communication across cultures.* New York: HarperCollins.

Mastro, D. E. (2003). A social identity to understanding the impact of television messages. *Communication Monographs, 70,* 98-113.

McCroskey, J. C. (1977). Oral communication apprehension: A summary of recent theory and research. *Human Communication Research, 4,* 78-96.

Miller, G., Boster, F., Roloff, M., & Seibold, D. (1977). Compliance-gaining strategies: A typology and some findings concerning effects of situational differences. *Communication Monographs, 44,* 37-51.

Neuliep, J. W. (2002). Assessing the Reliability and Validity of the Generalized Ethnocentrism Scale. *Journal of Intercultural Communication Research, 31,* 201-215.

Neuliep, J. W., Chaudoir, M., & McCroskey, J. C. (2001). A cross-cultural comparison of ethnocentrism among Japanese and United States college students. *Communication Research Reports, 18,* 137-146.

Neuliep, J. W., & McCroskey, J. C. (1997). A development of intercultural and interethnic communication apprehension scales. *Communication Research Reports, 14,* 145-156.

Neuliep, J. W., & Ryan, D. J. (1998). The influence of intercultural communication apprehension and socio-communicative orientation on uncertainty reduction during initial cross-cultural interaction. *Communication Quarterly, 46,* 88-99.

Orbe, M. P., & Warren, K. T. (2000). Different standpoints, different realities: Race, gender, and perceptions of intercultural conflict. *Communication Quarterly, 48,* 51-57.

Popp, D., Donovan, R. A., Crawford, M., Marsh, K. L., & Peele, M. (April, 2003). Gender, race, and speech style stereotypes. *Sex Roles,* 317-325.

Salari, S. (2002). Invisible in aging research: Arab Americans, Middle Eastern immigrants, and Muslims in the United States. *The Gerontologist, 42,* 580-588.

Taylor, D. M., & Porter, L. E., (1994). A multicultural view of stereotyping. In W. J. Lonner & R. Malpass (Eds.), *Psychology and culture,* (pp. 85-90). Boston: Allyn & Bacon.

Toale, M. C. & McCroskey, J. C. (2001). Ethnocentrism and trait communication apprehension as predictors of interethnic communication apprehension and use of relational maintenance strategies in interethnic communication. *Communication Quarterly, 49,* 70.

Uba, L. (1994). *Asian-Americans: Personality patterns, identity, and mental health.* New York: The Guilford Press.

U.S. Census. (2004). Projected population of the U.S. by race. Retrieved on May, 2 2004, from http://www.census.gov/ipc/www/usinterimproj/natprojtab01a.pdf.

Weitz, R., & Gordon, L. (1993). Images of Black women among Anglo college students. *Sex Roles, 28,* 19-34.

Appendix A (for sample research prospectus)

Ethnocentrism Scale

This is the Revised Ethnocentrism Scale. Of the 22 items, 15 are scored. The other seven are included to balance the number of positively and negatively worded items. You can expect an alpha reliability estimate in the range of .80 and .90 in most cases. For validity information on this scale see: Neuliep, J. W. (2002). Assessing the Reliability and Validity of the Generalized Ethnocentrism Scale. *Journal of Intercultural Communication Research, 31,* 201-215.

Below are items that relate to the cultures of different parts of the world. Work quickly and record your first reaction to each item. There are no right or wrong answers. Please indicate the degree to which you agree or disagree with each item using the following five-point scale:

Strongly Disagree = 1; Disagree = 1; Neutral = 3; Agree = 4; Strongly Agree = 5;

_____1. Most other cultures are backward compared to my culture.

_____2. My culture should be the role model for other cultures.

_____3. People from other cultures act strange when they come to my culture.

_____4. Lifestyles in other cultures are just as valid as those in my culture.

_____5. Other cultures should try to be more like my culture.

_____6. I am not interested in the values and customs of other cultures.

_____7. People in my culture could learn a lot from people in other cultures.

_____8. Most people from other cultures just don't know what's good for them.

_____9. I respect the values and customs of other cultures.

_____10. Other cultures are smart to look up to our culture.

_____11. Most people would be happier if they lived like people in my culture.

_____12. I have many friends from different cultures.

_____13. People in my culture have just about the best lifestyles of anywhere.

_____14. Lifestyles in other cultures are not as valid as those in my culture.

_____15. I am very interested in the values and customs of other cultures.

_____16. I apply my values when judging people who are different.

_____17. I see people who are similar to me as virtuous.

_____18. I do not cooperate with people who are different.

_____19. Most people in my culture just don't know what is good for them.
_____20. I do not trust people who are different.
_____21. I dislike interacting with people from different cultures.
_____22. I have little respect for the values and customs of other cultures.

Recode questions 4, 7, and 9 with the following format:

    1=5
    2=4
    3=3
    4=2
    5=1

Drop questions 3, 6, 12, 15, 16, 17, 19.

After you have recoded the previous questions, add all of the responses to the remaining 15 items together to get your composite ethnocentrism score.

Source of original scale: Neuliep, J. W., & McCroskey, J. C. (1997).The development of a U.S. and generalized ethnocentrism scale. *Communication Research Reports, 14,* 385-398.

Appendix B (for sample research prospectus)

Vignettes

Please read the following vignettes and respond to the following questions.

1. Since you are early to meet a friend for lunch, you decide to sit outside and enjoy the nice weather at a coffee shop to pass the time. As you finish your beverage outside, you notice that you forgot to wear your watch and you need to know what time it is; you don't want to keep your friend waiting. There is a person similar to you in dress and age sitting a few tables away drinking coffee.

Based on this scenario, please circle below whether you strongly disagree, disagree, are undecided, agree, or strongly agree that you would feel anxious or nervous to ask the person for the time if the person sitting outside was:

African-American

1	2	3	4	5
Strongly Disagree	Disagree	Undecided	Agree	Strongly Agree

Asian

1	2	3	4	5
Strongly Disagree	Disagree	Undecided	Agree	Strongly Agree

Caucasian

1	2	3	4	5
Strongly Disagree	Disagree	Undecided	Agree	Strongly Agree

Hispanic

1	2	3	4	5
Strongly Disagree	Disagree	Undecided	Agree	Strongly Agree

Middle Eastern

1	2	3	4	5
Strongly Disagree	Disagree	Undecided	Agree	Strongly Agree

2. While visiting a different U.S. city, you become disoriented while looking for your hotel. You know you are close, but are not sure which direction you need to walk to get to the address. There is a person sitting on a bench a few feet away from you who looks similar in age and dress to you.

Based on this scenario, please circle below whether you strongly disagree, disagree, are undecided, agree, or strongly agree that you would feel anxious or nervous to ask the person on the bench for directions the person was:

African-American

1	2	3	4	5
Strongly Disagree	Disagree	Undecided	Agree	Strongly Agree

Asian

1	2	3	4	5
Strongly Disagree	Disagree	Undecided	Agree	Strongly Agree

Caucasian

1	2	3	4	5
Strongly Disagree	Disagree	Undecided	Agree	Strongly Agree

Hispanic

1	2	3	4	5
Strongly Disagree	Disagree	Undecided	Agree	Strongly Agree

Middle Eastern

1	2	3	4	5
Strongly Disagree	Disagree	Undecided	Agree	Strongly Agree

Appendix C

SURVEY

Please fill in the blanks below with the number that you feel best indicates how much you agree with the following statements.

1 = strongly disagree
2 = disagree
3 = undecided
4 = agree
5 = strongly agree

My perceptions of African-Americans have been largely shaped by interactions that I have had with African-American people who are
___ Friends
___ Family members
___ Coworkers/classmates
___ On television
___ Other

My perceptions of Asians have been largely shaped by interactions that I have had with Asian people who are
___ Friends
___ Family members
___ Coworkers/classmates
___ On television
___ Other

My perceptions of Caucasians have been largely shaped by interactions that I have had with Caucasian people who are
___ Friends
___ Family members
___ Coworkers/classmates
___ On television
___ Other

My perceptions of Hispanics have been largely shaped by interactions that I have had with Hispanic people who are
___ Friends
___ Family members
___ Coworkers/classmates
___ On television
___ Other

My perceptions of Middle Easterners have been largely shaped by interactions that I have had with Middle Eastern people who are
___ Friends
___ Family members
___ Coworkers/classmates
___ On television
___ Other

Appendix E

Quantitative Research Paper

Running head: CANCER HEALTH INFORMATION SOURCES

Health Information Sources of Individuals with Cancer and Their Family Members

Loretta Pecchioni

Louisiana State University

Lisa Sparks[1]

George Mason University

1. Requests for reprints should be sent to Lisa Sparks, Department of Communication, George Mason University, MS3D6, Fairfax, VA 22030, lsparks@gmu.edu.

Abstract

The purpose of this study was to understand health information sources of individuals and families impacted by a cancer diagnosis. Overall, the findings support the Freimuth et al. (1989) model of health information acquisition. The cancer patients and family members who participated reported having significantly more health information along the continuum of cancer care, from causes to prevention, after a cancer diagnosis. Although a wide variety of interpersonal and mediated information sources are available, participants reported that the only consistently (88.1%) used source of information was doctors. The most **important** information sources were, in descending order, doctors, family members, nurses, friends, the Internet, other medical personnel, and other patients. Individuals, however, were most **satisfied** with family and friends, as sources of information, followed by nurses, other patients, and doctors. Patients and family members rated the **importance** of and their **satisfaction** with various information sources differently. Patients rated nurses, other medical personnel, and support groups as more important than did family members, while patients were significantly more satisfied with doctors and nurses, and family members were significantly more satisfied with the Internet.

Health Information Sources of Individuals with Cancer
and Their Family Members

In 2000, more than 1 million new cancers were diagnosed in the United States, and over half of those individuals were expected to die from the disease (American Cancer Society, 2000). However, survival rates are increasing, leading to a shift from coping with dying from cancer to coping and living with cancer (Baider, Cooper, & Kaplan De-Nour, 1996; Ell, Nishimoto, Mantell, & Hamovitch, 1988). Thus, it is essential that we understand how individuals affected by cancer gather relevant information to help in the coping process. The diagnosis of cancer not only affects the person with the disease, but also affects that person's family and friends (Baider, et al., 1996; Ferrell & Dow, 1996; Ferrell & Ferrell, 1998; Northouse & Peters-Golden, 1993; Wellisch, 1998). Thus, millions of family members are also living with this disease. However, little research has examined the ways by which family members and those diagnosed with cancer gather and obtain relevant and useful cancer information.

Freimuth, Stein, and Kean (1989) proposed a simple decision-point model to summarize and account for the variety of factors that influence health information acquisition. A stimulus (e.g., experiencing symptoms) generates a need to evaluate an individual's current knowledge based on previous exposure through interpersonal and mediated sources. If the individual decides that s/he does not have sufficient knowledge, then s/he will establish, at least implicitly, a set of information goals and weigh the costs and benefits of seeking additional information. For example, an individual with negative attitudes toward prognosis may delay a visit to the doctor (Freimuth et al., 1989). As the individual seeks information regarding symptoms that are being experienced, family and friends will encourage the individual to see a doctor about these symptoms.

If the individual goes to the doctor and receives a positive diagnosis, then the need for further information may be enhanced (Freimuth et al., 1989). Now the needed information is in regard to treatment options, survivability, and coping with physical and emotional reactions. At this point, however, several factors influence the nature of the information-seeking process, including the individual's trait desire for information in general, the level of interest the individual has in participating in the decision-making process regarding his/her health, the prognosis, the perceived adequacy of the current information, and demographic characteristics, such as age and education level. Throughout this process, not only is the individual who is experiencing the disease driven to acquire more information, but so are significant others in that person's life who have been informed about the diagnosis.

This study tests the Freimuth et al. (1989) model of health information acquisition, particularly in regard to the salience of information-seeking following a diagnosis and the use of information sources. In addition, this study extends that research in three ways. First, the Freimuth et al. (1989) study focused on an evaluation of the use and satisfaction with a hotline/referral service (specifically, the Cancer Information Service). This study asked participants about the range of information sources they used. Second, this study asked participants not only about their use of a variety of information sources, but the importance of, and their satisfaction with, each source. Third, Freimuth et al. (1989) mentioned the potential for the use of new technology in disseminating health-related information, and this study updates our knowledge of the Internet as a source of cancer-related information.

Review of Literature

Information Sources

Health care consumers acquire a wide range of information via communication (Kreps, O'Hair, & Clowers, 1994). People are bombarded with hundreds of messages everyday — from the media, health care professionals, their friends and family, coworkers and other individuals in their community, and from themselves. In order to simply get through the day, individuals must be selective about which messages receive their attention (Kelly, 1955; Delia, O'Keefe, & O'Keefe, 1982). Information regarding health is no exception. As Freimuth et al. (1989) pointed out people see advertisements on television, in magazines and newspapers, and hear them on the radio; other people in their lives discuss health-related information along with their concerns and worries; and, individuals send themselves health-related messages, saying to themselves, "I really should cut down on the fat in my diet" or "I need to start getting more exercise." Concern with how individuals obtain and use health information is increasing as health care policies push for citizens to take greater responsibility for their own health (Atkin & Arkin, 1990; Friemuth, Edgar, & Fitzpatrick, 1993; O'Keefe, Boyd, & Brown, 1998; Parrott, Kahl, & Maibach, 1995; Rogers, 1994).

Because many health campaigns attempt to prevent a variety of cancers — skin, prostate, breast, colorectal —have all received considerable attention in recent years, individuals often have baseline knowledge about the prevention and symptoms of these cancers (Freimuth et al., 1989). Most individuals, however, have generally negative images of cancer as a diagnosis — that it is a death sentence, or that the treatment is worse than the disease. Many of us have heard stories about individuals vomiting and being nauseated from chemotherapy, and some of us have experienced such scenarios, although these extreme attitudes toward cancer are changing (Baider et al., 1996; Ell et al., 1988).

While consumers tend to turn to doctors for needed information, the physician is not the only source of information. For example, family caregivers responsible for distributing medications to older family members with dementia report seeking information from pharmacists, nurses, neighbors, and the media, as well as physicians (Travis, Sparks-Bethea, & Winn, 2000). An individual undergoing radiation or chemotherapy treatment is likely to encounter a variety of technical support personnel who, at a minimum, will explain specific procedures that they administer. In some facilities, nurses and social workers are specifically assigned to discuss treatment and recovery issues (Beebe, 1995). In addition, organizations and associations concerned with specific diseases provide pamphlets and flyers, maintain Web sites on the Internet, operate information and referral hotlines, and advertise in the media. Pharmaceutical companies have recently been allowed to advertise directly to patients, encouraging them to ask their doctors about the benefits of a certain drug. Individuals may discuss their disease with other patients, either informally in waiting rooms or more formally in support groups (Freimuth et al., 1989). Individuals with symptoms and diagnoses often turn to family and friends who have specialized medical training when they are available (Freimuth et al., 1989). However, individuals also gain health-related knowledge through informal conversations with their peers who are not trained professionals (Bongarts & Watkins, 1996; Remez, 1996; Schuler, Choque, & Rance, 1994; Valente, Poppe, & Merritt, 1996; Valente & Saba, 1998).

Salience

Whether and which health-related messages will be attended to and acted upon, however, will depend to a large extent on how salient that information is to the individual (Freimuth et al., 1989). For example, an individual who is feeling ill or notices a lump is more likely to be attuned to information regarding possible explanations for these conditions. Typically, people turn first to their families and loved ones regarding their symptoms, who in turn encourage the individual to go to a doctor for a medical check-up (Adams & Kerner, 1982; Freimuth et al., 1989).

When the doctor has to break bad news and pronounces, "You have cancer," the individual reacts with shock, worry, concern, and even relief (Fallowfield, Hall, Maquire, & Baum, 1990; Houts, Rusenas, Simmonds, & Hufford, 1991). This individual is now motivated to seek out more information. Those people close to the individual may be similarly motivated to seek additional information so that they can allay their own fears and provide comfort to the individual who has been diagnosed with cancer (Freimuth et al., 1989; Houts et al., 1991).

Following a diagnosis, the vast majority of cancer patients want to be informed about their illness (Meredith et al., 1996) and report that having information helps them to cope with their disease, both physically and psychologically (Casslith, Zupkis, Sutton-Smith, & March, 1980; Fallowfield, Ford, & Lewis, 1995; Meredith et al., 1996). One problem, however, is sorting through the vast amount of information available to identify that which is the most relevant (Freimuth et al., 1989).

Motivation to Seek Information

Not all individuals have the same drive to seek out health-related information, even when that need has been made salient (Freimuth et al., 1989). Factors that influence an individual's motivation to seek additional information include his/her trait level of desire for information in general, the level of interest the individual has in participating in any health-related decisions, the prognosis for the disease, the perceived adequacy of current information, and demographic characteristics of the individual.

Many people have a high desire for as much information as possible in order to cope with the unknown (Jones et al., 1999; Meredith et al., 1996; National Cancer Alliance, 1996). Other individuals, however, would prefer not to have too much information, and are less likely to actively seek out more information. In spite of different levels of desire for seeking out information, Leydon et al. (2000) found that patients' primary need for information related to their doctors' ability to treat their disease. Once this need was fulfilled, they did not feel a continuing need to seek information regarding treatment options.

Another individual factor that may influence a patient's drive to seek more information is that patient's desire to be actively involved in his/her treatment decisions. As Freimuth et al., (1989) pointed out, the move toward greater patient involvement requires that patients be better informed. While several factors may play a role in limiting a patient's involvement, the patient's perception of a lack of information is a key element in limiting his or her ability to feel capable of taking an active role (Blanchard, Labrecque, Ruckdeschel, & Blanchard, 1988; Casselith et al., 1980; Degner et al., 1997; Hack, Degner, & Dyck, 1994; Degner & Sloan, 1992; Sutherland, Llewellyn-Thomas, Lockwood, Trichler, & Till, 1989).

The particular diagnosis may lead to varying levels of information-gathering (Friemuth et al., 1989). Those individuals in the later stages of an incurable cancer may decide that little research is needed because the cancer is at such an advanced stage that not much can be done to extend their life. In contrast, an individual who is diagnosed in the early stages of a curable cancer might be more apt to participate in the research process because the likelihood of curing the cancer and being able to live a healthy life is often very good.

Another factor influencing the search process is the evaluation of the adequacy of current information (Freimuth et al., 1989). Some individuals may find the search process confusing and overwhelming and experience technical information overload, especially if that information is contradictory. An individual may decide that the contradictory nature of the information is too high of a cost and will not continue the search for clarifying information. On the other hand, an individual may decide that the contradictory nature of the information requires a more diligent search in order to make sense out of the information.

Certain demographic characteristics may also influence the information-seeking process. O' Keefe, Boyd, and Brown (1998) found that for general health care information, older and more-educated individuals tend to learn more from newspapers and magazines, whereas younger and less-educated individuals get more information from television. Examining information-seeking among cancer patients, Turk-Charles, Meyerowitz, and Gatz (1997) found that information-seeking from doctors and nurses declined with age, but found no differences across age groups in information-seeking from newspapers, television, and friends. Prior research indicates that women receive more health care information from providers than do men (Weisman & Teitelbaum, 1989), and prefer using more formal channels (Johnson & Meischke, 1991).

Satisfaction with Information

Although the majority of cancer patients want as much information as possible, they are not always satisfied with the information that they receive. Individuals who report lower levels of satisfaction with the information they receive are more likely to be depressed or highly anxious about their diagnosis, especially when they receive contradictory information from different health care professionals (Jones, et al., 1999). Therefore, the amount of information does not successfully predict satisfaction with that information. While patients want information, they want information that they can assimilate, that is relevant and consistent.

Hypothesis and Research Questions

With the large number of individuals impacted, directly as a patient or indirectly through a loved one's diagnosis, and the serious consequences of a cancer diagnosis, it is important that we understand the information-seeking process of such individuals. This study examines the sources of information used by cancer patients and their family members, focusing on their perceptions of the importance of, and their satisfaction with, these information sources.

When presented with a stimulus, individuals seek more information related to the issue at hand (Freimuth, et al., 1989). Therefore, individuals, whether patients or their family members, should have more information after a cancer diagnosis than before, which leads to the following hypothesis:

H1:   Individuals will report having more information regarding cancer after they or a family member has received a cancer diagnosis than before.

Because of the wide range of both interpersonal and mediated information sources available, individuals will have many options from which to choose. This fact leads to the following research question:

RQ1: What health information sources do individuals, both as patients and family members, report using after receiving a diagnosis of cancer?

Individuals may find different health information sources to be more important or more satisfying than others, which leads to the following research questions:

RQ2: How do individuals, both patients and their family members, rate the relative importance of different health information sources?

RQ3: How do individuals, both patients and their family members, rate their satisfaction with different health information sources?

In addition, because the patient is dealing directly with health-related concerns and the family member is dealing with these issues secondhand, they may rate various health information sources differently, which leads to the following research questions:

RQ4: Do patients and their family members rate the importance of different health information sources differently?

RQ5: Do patients and their family members rate their satisfaction with different health information sources differently?

Methods and Procedures

Participants

Students received extra credit in a course at a large public university in the mid-Atlantic states for recruiting participants. Participants completed the survey at their own convenience, and the students returned the surveys to the faculty member. Of the 168 successfully completed surveys, 50% (n = 84) of the participants were individuals who had been diagnosed with cancer, and 50% (n = 84) were family members of such individuals. For all participants, the average age was 40.61 years (sd = 17.53, range 11-91). As a group, those who had cancer were older (average age = 48.46 years, sd = 16.32) than the family members (average age = 32.76 years, sd = 15.08). Almost two-thirds (73.8%) of the participants were female, while 66.7% were of European-American descent, 16.1% were African-American, 7.1% were Asian-American, 5.4% were from outside of the United States, 2.4% were Hispanic, 1.8% were Mexican-American, and 0.6% were Native-American. On average, the participants were well educated, with 21.5% having graduate hours or advanced degrees, and another 60.7% having some college hours or a baccalaureate degree. Nearly half (47.6%) of the participants were married and over one-third (36.9%) were single. For those participants who were family members of the person with cancer, nearly half (46.4%) reported that they were grandchildren, nieces, nephews, cousins or step-relatives of that person, over one-fourth (29.8%) were children of that person, 8.3% were spouses, 8.3% were siblings, and 7.1% were parents.

Survey Instrument

The survey asked for basic demographic information about the respondent and, for those individuals who were reporting on a family member's illness, demographic information about the family member, and information about the diagnosis, such as type of cancer, when diagnosed, and the prognosis. To gather data on the use, importance of, and satisfaction with different sources, participants were directed to think about the diagnosis of this particular individual. Participants were asked to think about the information they had about this <u>specific</u> type of cancer and to indicate the amount of information they had before and after the diagnosis. To measure the amount of information individuals had, respondents indicated on a scale from 1 (no information) to 5 (lots of information) how much information they had before and after the diagnosis, regarding causes and prevention, symptoms, and treatment options. The next section of the survey provided a list of several information sources, and participants were asked to rate the importance of each information source in this particular case. To measure level of importance, respondents circled the appropriate number on a scale from 1 (extremely important) to 5 (not very important). After these values were entered into the database, they were reverse coded so that larger numbers indicated greater importance. Participants were then asked to rate their satisfaction with each of these information sources by responding to a list of questions for each source. To measure satisfaction, the respondents rated each source from 1 to 7 on seven semantic differential scales, which were counterbalanced. The semantic differentials were understandable-confusing, easily available-difficult to find, useful-not useful, comforting-distressing, helpful-not helpful, trouble free-frustrating, and presented in a caring way-presented in a cold way. After these values were entered into the database, four of the items were reverse coded so that higher values for all items indicated greater satisfaction. Factor analysis revealed the seven semantic differential scales consistently loaded into one factor and were highly correlated for all information sources (reliability ranged from a low of .73 for magazines to a high of .89 for support groups). Therefore, summary scores were developed for each information source, with 7 being the lowest value and 49 being the highest, with higher values indicating greater satisfaction.

Results

Hypothesis one tested if salience affected information-seeking; therefore participants were asked how much information they had before and after the diagnosis. As predicted, participants reported having significantly more information after the diagnosis in all areas from causes and prevention (before diagnosis mean knowledge = 2.32, sd = 1.14; after diagnosis mean knowledge = 3.01, sd = 1.11, paired sample t = 15.33, p < .001) to symptoms (before diagnosis mean knowledge = 2.27, sd = 1.07; after diagnosis mean knowledge = 3.99, sd = .98, paired sample t = 17.86, p < .001) to treatment options (before diagnosis mean knowledge = 2.30, sd = 1.09; after diagnosis mean knowledge = 4.11, sd = .93, paired sample t = 17.51, p < .001). Individuals apparently did seek more information as the need became more salient following a diagnosis.

Research question one addressed which information sources would be used among the vast array of information sources available. The vast majority of individuals (88.1%) reported doctors as a source of information. About half of the participants indicated that they had used flyers (53.0%), the Internet (50.6%), family members (47.6%), and nurses (44.6%). More-rarely reported sources of information were friends (33.9%), magazines (32.7%), television (29.8%), other patients (29.2%), newspapers (28.6%), other medical personnel (28.0%), formal support groups (11.3%), radio (11.3%), and hotlines (5.4%).

Research question two asked about the relative **importance** of information sources (Table 1). An overall F-test indicated that participants rated the importance of the various information sources as significantly different ($F_{1,114}$ = 17.24, p < .001). The Games-Howell post-hoc multiple comparison procedure identified which sources were different from each other. Doctors were rated as the most important source of information, followed by family members, nurses, friends and the Internet, other medical personnel, and other patients (see Table 1).

Research question three asked about the relative **satisfaction** with each information source (Table 2). An overall F-test indicated that participants rated their satisfaction with the various information sources as significantly different ($F_{1,114}$ = 16.37, p < .001). The Games-Howell post-hoc multiple comparison procedure identified which sources were different from each other. Participants were most-satisfied with family, then friends, followed by nurses, other patients, and doctors (see Table 2).

Research question four asked if patients and family members rated the **importance** of various information sources differently. A series of ANOVAs was conducted to compare the ratings on importance of information sources between patients and family members. Patients rated nurses ($F_{1,154}$ = 3.97, p < .05), other medical personnel ($F_{1,143}$ = 15.64, p < .001) and support groups ($F_{1,130}$ = 10.58, p = .001) significantly higher than did family members. No other differences were significant.

Research question five asked if **patients and family members rated their satisfaction with the various information sources differently**. Again, a series of ANOVAs was conducted to compare the satisfaction of patients and family members with the different sources of information. Patients were more satisfied with doctors ($F_{1,149}$ = 3.98, p < .05) and nurses ($F_{1,135}$ = 5.65, p < .05), while family members were more satisfied with the Internet ($F_{1,114}$ = 4.20, p < .05). No other differences were significant.

Discussion

Overall, the findings from this study support the Freimuth et al. (1989) model of health information acquisition. As predicted, individuals report having more information once the need for information is made salient, that is, following their own or a family member's diagnosis of cancer.

The Freimuth et al. (1989) study focused on evaluating the use of, and satisfaction with, a hotline/referral source. This study suggests that such sources may play a relatively minor role in the acquisition of cancer-related information, as participants in this study reported interpersonal sources as being more important than mediated sources, with doctors being the most important source of information, followed by family and nurses. Overall, interpersonal sources were more-frequently accessed than mediated sources, with the exception of flyers, which are typically distributed by the doctor and usually address a particular disease or treatment. While flyers were reported as the most-frequently accessed mediated form, they were not significantly more important than the Internet. When Freimuth et al. (1989) developed their model, they commented on the burgeoning use of technology, but could not predict its effect on information-seeking. The findings of this study suggest that the Internet has become a useful tool to gather information, at least for a segment of the population; possibly serving as a supplemental informational source to interpersonal sources, rather than replacing such important relational sources (Baum & Yoder, 2002; Campbell & Wright, 2002; Lindberg, 2002; Wright, 2000, 2002). Somewhat surprising was the finding that relatively few patients reported using formal support groups, and neither patients nor family members used information and referral hotlines to a large extent.

The Friemith et al. (1989) model focused on the use of information sources. This study extended that model by examining both the importance of, and the satisfaction with, different information sources. Although doctors were reported to be the most important information sources, participants were not always as satisfied with them as they were with other sources. In fact, seven participants (4.2%) spontaneously commented that they were reporting on their satisfaction with a second doctor. These participants indicated that they had been particularly dissatisfied with the first doctor they had seen and had changed doctors in order to find one with whom they felt more comfortable. As one 58-year-old woman wrote, "I was so disgusted when I found out that the symptoms I had complained about for 2 years were serious and had been dismissed by this insensitive ob-gyn, I just had to find someone I could trust." The important role that doctors play in providing information cannot be dismissed, therefore, because individuals who are dissatisfied with one doctor will move on to another who will more successfully meet their needs. Participants in this study appear to be taking charge of their own health to the extent that they can, which supports prior research (see e.g., Atkin & Arkin, 1990; Friemuth, Edgar, & Fitzpatrick, 1993; O'Keefe, Boyd, & Brown, 1998; Parrott, Kahl, & Maibach, 1995; Rogers, 1994).

Nearly one half (47.6%) of respondents noted that they particularly turned to family and friends who had some level of health-related knowledge such as doctors, nurses, pharmacists, or other medical personnel. Some of these individuals, however, were not in health care professions, but were individuals who had a previous personal experience with a related illness. For example, a 45-year-old man reported he turned to his older brother who had also been diagnosed with prostate cancer two years earlier. These participants reported being most satisfied with family and friends, probably because these significant others are the most supportive and the most available. This finding supports prior research indicating that many individuals gain health-related knowledge through their life experiences and informal conversations with their peers who are often not trained professionals (Bongarts & Watkins, 1996; Remez, 1996; Schuler, Choque, & Rance, 1994; Valente, Poppe, & Merritt, 1996; Valente & Saba, 1998). One 36-year-old woman noted, however that "some of my friends were really insensitive, they didn't understand, I decided they really weren't friends after all." Therefore, the nature of the social support network may be tested beyond satisfactory limits. Some individuals in the social support network may have "natural" tendencies to provide emotional support, while others may find the cancer diagnosis too frightening or upsetting in order to provide appropriate support to friends and family.

While patients and family members, generally, agreed on the importance of, and their satisfaction with, the different health information sources, patients reported that doctors, nurses, and support groups were more important to them. This finding probably reflects the fact that patients, in general, have more access to health care professionals and formal groups. This fact may be particularly true for the family members in this study, as the majority (68.2%) of them did not serve as primary caregivers and, therefore, would have been unlikely to attend medical visits with their family members. Patients also reported finding doctors and nurses as more satisfying sources of information. Again, this finding probably reflects their greater level of access to these sources.

Family members, compared to patients, reported the Internet as more-satisfying in their search for information. Because family members may have less access to the health professionals, they may need to make a greater effort to find the information they need through other means, including available mediated forms. Because most of these family members were not the primary caregiver, they were not only unlikely to attend medical visits with the patient, but also were unlikely to be able to get information directly from the attending physician through phone calls or emails, as physicians do not discuss patient health without explicit permission from the patient. For example, a physician is unlikely to divulge information to a niece who is concerned about her aunt's condition. As noted before, the family members in this sample were fairly young and also well educated, so they may be more technologically savvy and more likely to have easy access to the technology, suggesting a reason for their comfort with using the Internet, in particular.

The results of this analysis indicate several practical implications for health care practitioners, individuals diagnosed with cancer, and families affected by cancer. Health care practitioners need to understand not only their personal role in providing information, but how that information may reinforce or contradict the information already held by the cancer patient or his/her family member. Health care practitioners need to be prepared to tailor information to the needs of patients and their families. In addition, they may need to find ways to make this information more available not only to the patient and primary caregiver, but to the extended family network, as well. While health care professionals may not be able to make themselves directly available to all of these individuals, they may want to direct them to reliable, accessible, and useful sources.

When possible, family members of those diagnosed with cancer and individuals who have cancer seem to be taking their health into their own hands. Increasing reliance on managed care with its attendant shift in the direction of the health care consumer taking a more assertive approach toward gathering and understanding a variety of cancer-related health information may be reflected in these results. As a consequence, individuals need the skills necessary to identify relevant information and to evaluate, assimilate, and use that information in productive ways.

Limitations

A number of limitations exist to this study in terms of the methods used and the inferences that can be made about the nature of how people gather cancer-related health care information. Future studies must assess a broader range of individuals diagnosed with cancer and family members dealing with cancer, particularly because as age increases, the likelihood of getting cancer also increases and information-seeking strategies may be different for different age cohorts. Other limitations of this study include the use of a non-probability sample and the fact that the self-reports of perceived health care providers by participants may have been biased.

Future Studies and Conclusions

This analysis supports and extends the Freimuth et al. (1989) model, suggesting that we should continue to examine the factors that contribute to how individuals gather, use, and understand their cancer-related health care information. Future studies should examine the factors that lead to failure within the support network, so that we better understand when individuals will not be able to provide sufficient emotional support to cancer patients, and create opportunities for patients to receive sufficient support. The credibility of cancer-related health information sources should be assessed to determine if patients and their families are using accurate information. In addition, future studies should address the effect of information-seeking about cancer-related health issues from interpersonal channels on the Internet, such as chat rooms, as a source of health information. This study provides some important basic data about where individuals gather cancer-related health care information and the differences between patients and their family members.

By understanding how cancer patients and their families gather information, researchers and practitioners can now begin to more specifically create and communicate effective, credible, and accessible health care messages and information via appropriate and effective interpersonal and mediated channels. The next task, albeit a difficult one, is to direct the cancer health care consumer to credible and reliable cancer information sources.

References

Adams, M., & Kerner, J. (1982). Evaluation of promotional strategies to solve the problem of underutilization of a breast examination center in a New York City black community. In C. Mettlin & G. P. Murphy (Eds.), *Issues in cancer screening and communications*. New York: Alan R. Liss, Inc.

Atkin, C., & Arkin, E. B. (1990). Issues and initiatives in communicating health information. In C. Atkin & L. Wallack (Eds.), *Mass communication and public health* (pp. 13-40). Newbury Park, CA: Sage.

Baider, L., Cooper, C., & Kaplan De-Nour, A. (1996). Introduction. In L. Baider, C. Cooper, & A. Kaplan De-Nour (Eds.), *Cancer and the family* (pp. xvii-xviii). West Sussex: John Wiley.

Baum, E. E., & Yoder, C. (2002). Senior support on-line. In R. W. Morrell (Ed.), *Older adults, health information, and the World Wide Web*, (pp. 187-199). Mahwah, NJ: Lawrence Erlbaum Associates.

Beebe, S. A. (1995). Nurses' perception of beeper calls: Implications for resident stress and patient care. *Archives of Pediatrics & Adolescent Medicine, 149*, 187-191.

Blanchard, C. G., Labrecque, M. S., Ruckdeschel, J. C., & Blanchard, E. B. (1988). Information and decision-making preferences of hospitalized adult cancer patients. *Social Science & Medicine, 27*, 1139-1145.

Bongaarts, J., & Watkins, S. (1996). Social interactions and contemporary fertility transitions. *Population and Development Review, 22*, 639-682.

Campbell, K., & Wright, K. B. (2002). On-line support groups: An investigation of relationships among source credibility, dimensions of relational communication, and perceptions of emotional support. *Communication Research Reports, 19*, 183-193.

Casselith, B. R., Zupkis, R. V., Sutton-Smith, K., & March, V. (1980). Information and participation preferences among cancer patients. *Annals of Internal Medicine, 92*, 832-836.

Degner, L. F., Kristjanson, L. J., Bowman, D., Sloan, J. A., Carriere, K. C., O'Neil, J., Bilodeau, B., Watson, P., & Mueller, B. (1997). Information needs and decisional preferences in women with breast cancer. *JAMA, The Journal of the American Medical Association, 277*, 1485-1492.

Degner, L. F., & Sloan, J. A. (1992). Decision making during serious illness: What role do patients really want to play? *Journal of Clinical Epidemiology, 45*, 941-950.

Delia, J., O'Keefe, B., & O'Keefe, D. (1982). The constructivist approach to communication. In F. E. X. Dance (Ed.), *Human communication theory* (pp. 147-191). New York: Harper & Row.

Ell, K., Nishimoto, R., Mantell, J., & Hamovitch, M. (1988). Longitudinal analysis of psychosocial adaptation among family members of patients with cancer. *Journal of Psychosomatic Research, 32*, 429-438.

Fallowfield, L., Ford, S., & Lewis, S. (1995). No news is not good news: Information preferences of patients with cancer. *Psycho-oncology, 4*, 197-202.

Fallowfield, L. J., Hall, A., Maguire, G. P., & Baum, M. (1990). Psychological outcomes of different treatment policies in women with early breast cancer outside a clinical trial. *British Medical Journal, 301*, 575-580.

Ferrell, B., & Dow, K. (1996). Portraits of cancer survivorship: A glimpse through the lens of survivors' eyes. *Cancer Practice, 4*, 76-80.

Ferrell, B., & Ferrell, B. (1998). The older patient. In J. Holland (Ed.), *Psycho-oncology* (pp. 839-844). New York: Oxford University Press.

Friemuth, V. S., Edgar, T., & Fitzpatrick, M. A. (1993). The role of communication in health promotion. *Communication Research, 20*, 509-516.

Freimuth, V. S., Stein, J. A., & Kean, T. J. (1989). *Searching for health information: The Cancer Information Service model*. Philadelphia, PA: University of Pennsylvania Press.

Hack, T. F., Degner, L. F., & Dyck, D. G. (1994). Relationship between preferences for decisional control and illness information among women with breast cancer: A quantitative and qualitative analysis. *Social Science & Medicine, 39*, 269-289.

Houts, P., Rusenas, I., Simmonds, M., & Hufford, D. (1991). Information needs of families of cancer patients: A literature review and recommendations. *Journal of Cancer Education, 6*, 225-261.

Johnson, J. D., & Meischke, H. (1992). Differences in evaluations of mass communication by the individual. In J. G. Blumler & E. Katz (Eds.), *The uses of mass communication* (pp. 19-32). Beverly Hills, CA: Sage.

Jones, R., Pearson, J., McGregor, S., Gilmour, W. H., Atkinson, J. M., Barrett, A., Cawsey, A., & McEwen, J. (1999). Cross sectional survey of patients' satisfaction with information about cancer. *British Medical Journal, 319,* 1247-1249.

Kelly, G. A. (1955). *The psychology of personal constructs.* New York: W. W. Norton.

Kreps, G., O'Hair, H. D., & Clowers, M. (1994). The influence of human communication on health outcomes. *American Behavioral Scientist, 38,* 248-257.

Leydon, G. M., Boulton, M., Moynihand, C., Jones, A., Mossman, J., Bouidioni, M., & McPherson, K. (2000). Cancer patients' information needs and information-seeking behaviour: In depth interview study. *British Medical Journal, 320,* 909-912.

Lindberg, D. A. B. (2002). Older Americans, health information, and the Internet. In R. W. Morrell (Ed.), *Older adults, health information, and the World Wide Web,* (pp. 13-19). Mahwah, NJ: Lawrence Erlbaum Associates.

Meissner, H. I., Potosky, A. L., & Convissor, R. (1992). How sources of health information relate to knowledge and use of cancer screening exams. *Journal of Community Health, 17,* 153-165.

Meredith, C., Symonds, P., Webster, L., Lamont, D., Pyper, E., Gillis, C. R., et al. (1996). Information needs of cancer patients in west Scotland: Cross sectional survey of patients' views. *British Medical Journal, 313,* 724-726.

National Cancer Alliance. (1996). *Patient-centred cancers services? What patients say.* Oxford, UK: National Cancer Alliance.

Northouse, L., & Peters-Golden, H. (1993). Cancer and the family: Strategies to assist spouses. *Seminars in Oncology Nursing, 9,* 74-82.

O'Keefe, G. J., Boyd, H. H., & Brown, M. R. (1998). Who learns preventative healthcare information from where: Cross-channel and repertoire comparisons. *Health Communication, 10,* 25-36.

Parrott, R. L., Kahl, M. L., & Maibach, E. W. (1995). Enabling health: Policy and administrative practices at a cross-road. In E. W. Maibach & R. L. Parrott (Eds.), *Designing health messages,* (pp. 270-283). Thousand Oaks, CA: Sage.

Remez, L. (1996). Both contraceptive use and unplanned births are common in Ecuador. *International Family Planning Perspectives, 22,* 85-86.

Rogers, E. M. (1995). *Diffusion of Innovations (4th).* New York: Free Press.

Schuler, S. R., Choque, M. E., & Rance, S. (1994). Misinformation, mistrust, and mistreatment: Family planning among Bolivian market women. *Studies in Family Planning, 25,* 211-221.

Sutherland, H. J., Llewellyn-Thomas, H. A., Lockwood, G. A., Trichler, D. L., & Till, J. E. (1989). Cancer patients: Their desire for information and participation in treatment decisions. *Journal of Society & Medicine, 82,* 260-263.

Travis, S. T., Sparks-Bethea, L., & Winn, P. (2000). Medication hassles reported by family caregivers of dependent elders. *Journal of Gerontology: Medical Sciences, 55A,* M412-416.

Turk-Charles, S., Meyerowitz, B. E., & Gatz, M. (1997). Age differences in information-seeking among cancer patients. *International Journal of Aging & Human Development, 45,* 85-98.

Valente, T. W., Poppe, P. R., & Merritt, A. P. (1996). Mass media generated interpersonal communication as sources of information about family planning. *Journal of Health Communication, 1,* 259-273.

Valente, T. W., & Saba, W. (1998). Mass media and interpersonal influence in a reproductive health communication in Bolivia. *Communication Research, 25,* 96-124.

Weisman, C. S., & Teitelbaum, M. A. (1989). Women and health care communication. *Patient Education and Counseling, 13,* 183-199.

Wellisch, D. (1998). Editorial introduction: Families and cancer. *Psycho-Oncology, 7,* 1-2.

Wright, K. B. (2002). Social support within an on-line cancer community: An assessment of emotional support, perceptions of advantages and disadvantages, and motives for using the community. *Journal of Applied Communication Research, 30,* 195-209.

Wright, K. B. (2000). Computer-mediated social support, older adults, and coping. *Journal of Communication, 50,* 100-118.

Table 1

All participants' ratings and statistical groupings of importance of health information sources.

Information Source	Importance Mean (sd) *n*	Group Membership
Doctor	4.64 (.87) *166*	A
Family	4.03 (1.27) *147*	B
Nurse	3.88 (1.28) *156*	B, C
Flyers	3.63 (1.14) *152*	C, D
Friends	3.49 (1.37) *140*	D, E
Internet	3.49 (1.33) *146*	D, E
Other medical personnel	3.32 (1.32) *145*	E
Other patients	3.26 (1.45) *140*	E
Magazines	2.70 (1.05) *142*	F
Television	2.69 (1.10) *143*	F
Newspaper	2.52 (1.03) *141*	G
Formal support groups	2.31 (1.29) *132*	G, H
Radio	2.26 (1.05) *136*	G, H
Hotline	2.18 (1.19) *130*	H

Note: The Games-Howell post-hoc multiple comparison procedure tests for significant differences between groups when the overall ANOVA is significant. Group means that are not significantly different are labeled by the same letter. Therefore, information sources with the same letter belong to the same grouping (are not significantly different within the grouping), and information sources that do not share a letter are significantly different from other groupings.

Table 2

All participants' ratings of satisfaction with, and statistical groupings of, health information sources.

Information Source	Satisfaction Mean (sd) *n*	Group Membership
Family	41.89 (7.78) *136*	A
Friends	40.68 (7.17) *119*	B
Nurse	38.31 (7.25) *137*	C
Other patients	38.13 (7.86) *112*	C, D
Doctor	37.57 (7.13) *151*	C, D
Flyers	36.14 (7.55) *137*	D
Formal support groups	34.67 (8.90) *79*	D, E
Internet	33.40 (7.91) *116*	E
Other medical personnel	32.93 (6.87) *100**	E, F
Magazines	31.37 (5.89) *119*	F
Television	30.51 (7.38) *116*	F, G
Newspaper	29.66 (6.60) *94**	G, H
Hotline	29.03 (7.69) *74*	G, H
Radio	26.55 (7.07) *92*	I

Note: The Games-Howell post-hoc multiple comparison procedure tests for significant differences between groups when the overall ANOVA is significant. Group means that are not significantly different are labeled by the same letter. Therefore, information sources with the same letter belong to the same grouping (are not significantly different within the grouping), and information sources that do not share a letter are significantly different from other groupings.

*Due to a copying error, 24 participants had pages that doubled the doctor and nurse scales and, thus, did not have responses for other medical personnel and newspapers, which is reflected in the lower number of responses to these sources.

Qualitative Research Paper

Running head: CULTURE & MEDICINE

Integrating Culture and Medicine

Eager Learner

Hometown University

Integrating Culture and Medicine

The cultural composition of the United States is rapidly changing. This growing ethnic diversity has placed new demands on the health care system for providing culturally sensitive care (Kernicki, 1997). Understanding the dynamics of culture in the patient-provider relationship is essential to developing effective methods for health care.

Culture is defined as a shared system of values, beliefs, and learned patterns of behaviors and is not simply defined by ethnicity (Carillo, Green, & Betancourt, 1999). These characteristics of culture shape the way people perceive their health and the way they interact with caregivers. A patient enters the physician's office with certain beliefs, concerns, and expectations about his or her illness and the medical encounter (Carillo et al., 1999). Therefore, physician recognition of the cultural context of patients' illnesses can be essential to a successful therapeutic relationship (Berger, 1998).

Payer (1989) describes the varieties of treatments prescribed by doctors in four Western countries: France, West Germany, Great Britain, and America. Basing her analysis on her own experiences, national studies, and interviews with people treated in these countries, she compares and contrasts medical techniques used by physicians in their treatments of certain medical conditions, and draws conclusions about the cultural cues taken by patients from these treatments. She characterizes each culture according to their stereotypical medical beliefs and practices. The French are thinkers, preferring to treat illnesses by developing logical ideas for treatments and following them out with little or no experimentation. They are also very focused on their livers in maintaining health. The Germans are romantics, focused on their hearts as the source of many of their maladies. The English are economic and very frugal in their diagnoses and medical expenditures. Americans, on the other hand, are doers who tend to "attack" medical problems very aggressively through the use of surgery and drugs. According to Payer, "while medicine benefits from a certain amount of scientific input, culture intervenes at every step of the way" (p. 26). Payer offers the following example:

> Blood pressure considered treatably high in the Unites States might be considered normal in England; and the low blood pressure treated with eighty-five drugs as well as hydrotherapy and spa treatments in Germany would entitle its sufferer to lower life insurance rates in the United States (p. 25).

Even though many medical conditions are examined and diagnosed differently depending on where the diagnosis is made, residents of these four countries have similar demographics and health statistics. The similar health statistics indicate that the medicine in these countries can be judged as equal. Although Payer points out that often all one needs to do to acquire a disease is cross a border into another country, she also emphasizes the importance of recognizing that the different methods and views of doctors allow possibilities for medical breakthroughs, and should be respected.

Although culture plays a significant role in determining effective approaches to treatment, there are also a number of other factors that must be emphasized. Social factors, such as socioeconomic status and education, and religious beliefs may play a role in shaping the conceptualization of an illness (Ware & Kleinman, 1992). Gender and age may also affect health practices and beliefs. For this reason, it is necessary to examine each person as an individual, not as a member of a stereotyped culture. Cultural groups are very heterogeneous, and individual members manifest different degrees of acculturation, making it difficult and even counterproductive to teach a culture as a whole (Carillo et al., 1999).

Methods

The following case studies offer additional evidence of culturally biased health beliefs and encourage further research about the connection between cultural beliefs and effective communication in the patient provider relationship. Four subjects were asked a series of questions via telephone interviews, email interviews, face-to-face interviews, and self-conducted interviews about what they believe causes and heals the common cold, cancer, depression, stomach aches, and arthritis. They were also asked what they believe causes good health and a long life, and what qualities they most appreciate in medical providers.

All of the test subjects currently reside in the United States and seek medical care from physicians in the U.S. Therefore, this study compares their cultural beliefs about health care to the beliefs of Americans in an effort to predict culturally determined communication difficulties that may arise during treatment from American health care providers. Three of the four test subjects are representative of two underlying cultural influences present in American society: Hispanic and German cultures. The fifth test subject is a control subject representational of typical American beliefs.

Subject 1 conducted a self-interview lasting fifteen minutes in her home. A telephone interview lasting thirty minutes was conducted for Subject 2 from her home. Subject 3 responded via email to the questions from her home, and participated in a follow-up interview over the telephone for twenty minutes. And Subject 4 was interviewed over the telephone for twenty minutes from his home. Notes were taken by the author for each interview. The data are illustrated in Table 1 and analyzed in the following section.

Subject 1 is the control subject. By conducting a self-interview, I have sought to provide a representational view of the typical American's health beliefs. I am a healthy, single, white, 26-year-old female who has resided in the Washington, D.C., metro area for one year. Previously, I had been a lifelong Louisiana resident. In my lifetime, I have had two major personal experiences with health care providers, other than annual check ups. The first experience occurred when I was 12 years old and had a severe reaction to medication. My liver began to shut down, and I was in the hospital for about three weeks. Then, when I was 20, I was hospitalized for two weeks after being involved in an accident that resulted in third-degree burns on my face and hands. During the former experience, I was misdiagnosed, and my condition worsened until I visited a different hospital. It was a very negative experience overall. During the later experience, I was 6,000 miles away from home, by myself, in Alaska. The doctors and nurses who cared for me were very compassionate and made extra efforts to make me feel better. In addition to these personal experiences, both of my parents had cancer; my mom had ovarian cancer thirteen years ago resulting in a hysterectomy, and twelve years ago, my dad had non-Hodgkins lymphoma. Both are currently in remission.

Subject 2 is a divorced, 42-year-old, Catholic woman of Hispanic descent; her father is Venezuelan, and her mother is Hispanic-American. She grew up in Venezuela and moved to Louisiana when she was 20, where she has lived ever since. This subject is physically healthy, but is currently being treated for frequent bouts of depression by a psychiatrist. She has no history of any serious physical medical conditions; however, she experienced losing her grandmother to brain cancer when she was 35.

Subject 3 is a healthy, 41-year-old, married, mother of two — a 17-year-old boy and a 19-year-old-girl. She is of Hispanic descent, and a practicing Catholic. Having grown up in El Salvador, she moved to Louisiana twenty-two years ago, when she married an American. She has lived there ever since. Subject three had two serious instances in which she was hospitalized. The first time was after a serious automobile accident in which she broke her arm and leg, and had several facial fractures. Her second hospitalization occurred five years ago when she was treated for kidney failure. She has also been hospitalized to give birth to her children. In comparing her experiences of hospitalization in El Salvador and the United States, Subject 3 stated that in America, the care is better because [health care providers] pay more attention to their patients. She also said, based on her own experiences, the overall treatment methods of physicians in El Salvador and America were the same.

Subject 4 is a healthy, 33-year-old, single man from Germany. Although he moved from Germany to Washington, D.C., five years ago, he frequently returns to Germany to visit his immediate family and friends, all of whom still live there. Subject 4 has never had any serious illness, but he did have surgery in Germany for a hernia twelve years ago. He does not practice any religion.

Discussion

According to Carrillo et al. (1999), social context is explored through four avenues, any of which may apply to a particular patient: 1) control over one's environment (such as financial resources and education), 2) changes in environment (such as migration), 3) literacy and language, and 4) social stressors and support systems. Social context, when applied to culture, can provide a route for both blending cultural beliefs and creating distinction among individuals within cultures. This is illustrated in the Subject responses.

Three central beliefs necessary for maintaining good health and a long life are shared by the test subjects; they are good eating habits, a good genetic make-up, and low exposure to pollution (see Table 1). Upon exploring what the term "good eating habits" means to each subject, it was determined that this idea varies. For Subject 1 and Subject 2, good eating habits referenced the types of food eaten, including a low-fat, high-fiber diet, consisting predominantly of fruits and vegetables. However, for Subjects 3 and 4, good eating habits are indicated by the amount and how often food is eaten, rather than the types of foods eaten. This difference is one indication of the language or meaning barriers that sometimes exist between different cultures. If an American caregiver asked either of the Hispanic subjects whether or not she had good eating habits, her yes or no answer may mean something different to the American. Further investigation about the types of food that these subjects eat would help determine if they had healthy eating habits by American standards.

Exposure to pollutants and chemicals was the reason attributed by all test subjects to be one of the main causes of cancer. All of the subjects listed chemotherapy and radiation therapy as treatment methods. This similarity of beliefs is inconsistent with previous studies in which Hispanic groups attributed the presence of cancer to sinful behavior (Berger, 1998). Based on the findings from this study, one could surmise that international cancer treatment has become more consistent. More likely, the similarity is due to the fact that cancer is just not a subject thought about much until one's adult years. Since all of the test subjects have spent the majority of their adult lives in the United States, their views of cancer and its treatment would have been influenced by American medical practices.

In fact, many of the beliefs expressed by the test subjects appear to be similar. Based on the fact that genetics has become a pervasive idea in Eestern cultures, it is no surprise that individuals from different cultures would share the view that their health is determined by their genetic make-up. Additionally, most people in America attribute the common cold to a virus, just as all of the test Subjects did. Explanations of these similarities in belief from people of different cultures can also be attributed to the fact that all of the Subjects are well educated (Carillo et al., 1999). Subjects 3 and 4 have attended some college, Subject 1 holds a Bachelors Degree, and Subject 2 holds a Ph.D. Additionally, the Test Subjects share similar socioeconomic backgrounds; they all come from middle- to upper-class families.

Even in the presence of relatively similar educational and socioeconomic backgrounds, other factors attribute to differences in cultural beliefs and values, such as religion. Subjects 2 and 3, both devout Catholics, expressed deep religious beliefs about their health. According to Kernicki (1997), the integration of physical, mental, and spiritual health is central to Hispanic culture. This statement is supported by responses given by Subject 2 and 3 to questions about the causes and treatments for certain ailments. For example, the subjects both share the belief that ultimately God is in control of one's health and how long people live, although they recognize that there are other scientific approaches that can be taken to maintain good health. Additionally, according to Subjects 2 and 3, prayer and spirituality are essential to the healing process. Spirituality is a key element present in the health beliefs of many Hispanics. It is essential that caregivers are aware of, and respect the role that, religion plays in health practices within cultures. Many patients integrate cultural health practices with reliance on medical practitioners. Knowledge and acknowledgement of these practices are important for physician-patient communication and may affect compliance with other medical procedures and treatments (Risser & Mazur, 1995).

Another cultural distinction exhibited by Hispanics is the belief that a state of health requires a balance between hot and cold (Risser & Mazur, 1995). According to Payer (1989) this balance of hot and cold is also a belief shared by the French and German cultures. Responses shown in Table 1 support the preceding findings. Subject 2 attributed the common cold and arthritis to exposing one's body to rapid fluctuation of temperature. Similarly, Subject 4 revealed that in Germany, people are very concerned about drafts, and the effects of the exposure to cold air on one's health and circulation. He stressed wearing gloves and keeping warm in cold weather to prevent arthritis.

Even though medical practices vary from country to country (Payer, 1989), it is possible for physicians from varying cultural backgrounds to develop positive relationships with culturally diverse patients through empathy, curiosity, and respect (Carrillo et al. 1999). When people from different cultural backgrounds visit doctors with a dissimilar cultural background, misinterpretations of meanings often occur due to many barriers—such as language, values, beliefs, sex, etc. The physician serves as the expert on the disease, whereas the patient experiences and expresses a unique illness and can be suffering from anxiety over the illness, further impeding the communicative process. Thus, even when the patient's and physician's sociocultural backgrounds are similar, substantial differences may exist still because of these separate perspectives. In order to develop effective treatment methods, physicians and caregivers must recognize the role that culture plays in communicating with their patients about health-related issues and find common ground to relate to, and be patient with, each individual.

Future Research

Future research should focus on a wider variety of cultures. Additionally, larger representative samples from each group should be interviewed to reveal more substantive data. Interviews of health care providers from varying backgrounds could also provide insight into physician-patient interactions. Additionally, a wider variety of health concerns should be examined through interviews and focus groups.

References

Berger, J. (1998). Culture and ethnicity in clinical care. *Archives of Internal Medicine, 158,* 2085-2092.

Carillo, J., & Green, A., & Betancourt, J. (1999). Cross-cultural primary care: A patient-based approach. *Annals of Internal Medicine, 130,* 829-834.

Kernicki, J. (1997). A multicultural perspective of cardiovascular disease. *Journal of Cardiovascular Nursing, 11(4),* 31-41.

Kerr, L., & Kerr, Jr., L. (2001). Screening tools for depression in primary care: The effects of culture, gender, and somatic symptoms on the detection of depression. *The Western Journal of Medicine, 175,* 349-353.

Payer, L. (1989). *Medicine and Culture.* New York: Penguin Books.

Risser, A., & Mazur, L. (1995). Use of folk remedies in a Hispanic population. *Archives of Pediatrics & Adolescent Medicine, 149,* 978-982.

Ware, N., & Kleinman, A. (1992). Culture and somatic experience: The social course of illness in neurasthenia and chronic fatigue syndrome. *Psychosom Med, 54,* 546-560.

Table 1

	Common Cold	Cancer	Depression	Stomachaches	Arthritis	Good Health	Long Life (Over 90 years)
Subject 1	**Cause:** Lowered immune systems allow virus to proliferate in cells, unhygienic practices, stress. **Heal:** Rest, vitamin C, immune system-boosting herbs or medication, drinking fluids.	**Cause:** Cell mutations: Due to genetic predispositions, environmental factors like pollutants, sun exposure, overuse of medications. **Heal:** Early detection and treatment, avoidance of unnecessary chemicals, good eating habits, positive outlook.	**Cause:** Overall negative feelings about life and our role in it, negative relationships with people and environmental surroundings, negative self-image, chemical imbalances. **Heal:** Change self-image by working to improve negative situations, surround self with positive people, talk about feelings/problems; if the following suggestion don't help, take medication.	**Cause:** Eating bad food, indigestion, stress, viruses. **Heal:** Eat good, fresh food, eat slowly, recognize why you are stressed by talking about it and take steps to alleviate the source of stress, wash hands and practice good hygiene.	**Cause:** Fluid retention, cold weather, excessive stress to joints. **Heal:** Stretching, yoga, hot baths, hot compresses, massage.	**Cause:** Eating healthy foods, exercising regularly, genetics, low-stress lifestyle, good hygiene, luck.	**Cause:** Having people close to you, having pets, body awareness, history of long life in family, staying in shape and active, a sense of self-confidence or self-sufficiency, being in good health.
Subject 2	**Cause:** Viruses, lowered immune system, lack of vitamins and sunlight, cold winter weather causes the body to become stressed. **Heal:** Feed a cold, sleep, drink a lot of fluids.	**Cause:** Cells mutate and are not disposed of properly, genetic predisposition, smoking, bad food. **Heal:** Can never be fully healed, just slowed down with chemotherapy and radiation.	**Cause:** Environment, stress, childhood experiences, chemical imbalances in brain, genetics and environment combining together in such a way to cause a negative reaction. **Heal:** Psychoanalysis, chemicals.	**Cause:** Stress, bad food, poison. **Heal:** Take antacid, relax, vomit.	**Cause:** Genetics, drafts. **Heal:** Wear gloves in cold weather, do not expose joints to drafts.	**Cause:** Eat healthy food, exercise at least 3 times per week.	**Cause:** Good health, good medical care, genetics, your environment, low exposure to chemicals and pollution, the amount of money you have, good hygiene, medical advances.

	Common Cold	Cancer	Depression	Stomachaches	Arthritis	Good Health	Long Life (Over 90 years)
Subject 3	**Cause:** A virus. **Heal:** Your body has to heal itself and let the virus run its course.	**Cause:** Chemicals and pollution in the environment. **Heal:** Chemo and radiation therapy, prayer.	**Cause:** Stress, chemical imbalances in the body. **Heal:** Faith in God.	**Cause:** Indigestion. **Heal:** Medicine.	**Cause:** Genetics. **Heal:** Medication.	**Cause:** Healthy eating habits, exercise, spirituality, genetics.	**Cause:** God determines how long you live.
Subject 4	**Cause:** The air, going outside in cold weather with wet hair causes you to catch a virus. **Heal:** Medicine, rubbing vapor rub on body.	**Cause:** Chemicals, pollution, smoking. **Heal:** Prayer, God.	**Cause:** Stress, yourself. **Heal:** Hang out with positive people, solve your problems by praying, and talking with family and friends.	**Cause:** Indigestion, bad food. **Heal:** Medicine, mansanillo tea (herbal remedy).	**Cause:** Rapid changes in temperature, i.e., washing your hands with warm water and then exposing them to cold. **Heal:** Massage therapy. Do not expose yourself to frequent temperature changes.	**Cause:** Good eating habits.	**Cause:** Maintaining good health, genetics.

Research Critique

Running head: FUNCTIONS OF TALK

Functions of Talk and Reports of Imagined Interactions (IIs)

During Engagement and Marriage

Stud Y. Us

Hometown University

Abstract

Honeycutt and Wiemann's (1999) research investigated individual differences within close relationships as a function of gender, marital status (engaged, married), and marital orientation (traditional, independent) on beliefs about talk. The authors took a functional approach to examining various characteristics of imagined interactions or self-talk in these relationships.

The purpose of this paper is to critique this article by evaluating the following research criteria: 1) adequacy of the literature review; and 2) the methodological procedures used to gather data. Results of this analysis indicate that although this research article was extremely thorough in conducting prior literature research, it failed in its methodological procedures used in gathering data.

Critique of Honeycutt and Wiemann's Analysis of Functions of Talk and
Reports of Imagined Interactions (IIs) During Engagement and Marriage

Basing their study on extensive prior research, Honeycutt and Wiemann (1999) examined the functions of talk and reports of imagined interactions (IIs) during engagement and marriage. The study showed that differences indeed exist in the functions of talk and in reports of imagined interactions, depending upon one's gender, marital status, and orientation. The purpose of this paper is to critique this article by evaluating the following research criteria: 1) adequacy of the literature review; and 2) the methodological procedures used to gather data.

Defining Research Criteria

This critique of Honeycutt and Wiemann's (1999) study examines the following research criteria: 1) adequacy of the literature review; and 2) the methodological procedures used to gather data. Using the research criteria discussed by Sparks (2005) and Frey, Botan, and Kreps (2000), each research criterion will be defined, described, and evaluated.

Adequacy of the Literature Review

Adequacy of the literature review is defined by the APA Publication Manual (2001) as a scholarly discussion of earlier work pertinent to the topic being studied. This review should not be an exhaustive history of an area of inquiry, but must assume that the audience has some knowledge of the field under study. The review should present a background of the problem clearly enough as to be understood by a wide professional audience. A logical continuity between earlier work and the current study must be presented (Publication Manual, 2001).

Methodology

The methodological procedures used to gather and analyze data must be appropriate for the problem being studied (Frey, et al., 2000). The design of an experiment, the methods used to gather data, and the tests used in analyzing the gathered data must all be selected so that validity, internal and external, as well as reliability is maximized. These choices must be made based on prior research in the area of study and on standard academic and scientific practice (Sparks, 2005).

Critique and Discussion

Adequacy of the Literature Review

Honeycutt and Wiemann (1999) appeared to have conducted an adequate review of prior literature before embarking upon their study. Thirty-four relevant studies were examined and utilized to design and conduct the study. A synopsis and discussion of prior research preceded each research question and hypothesis. For example, Honeycutt and Wiemann (1999) discussed the prior research of Clark and Delia (1979), Berger (1993, 1995), and Newton and Burgoon (1990) on instrumental objectives, relational management, and interpersonal influence. Honeycutt and Wiemann's first hypothesis followed this section and was stated as follows: "the functions of talk among engaged and married couples will reflect instrumental, relational management, and identity management strategies, including the sharing of interpersonal influence" (p. 9).

Methodology

Although Honeycutt and Wiemann's (1999) study was somewhat successful, many methodological procedures could have been improved. The study's method for gathering participants and data seemed to lack validity, reliability, and generalizability.

First, engaged participants were recruited from communication courses and marriage preparation workshops. Married couples were also recruited using a network sampling technique, or snowball sample. Researchers claim that this procedure limits the generalizability of the study and does not provide a representative sample (Frey, et al., 2000).

Future studies in this area might use better sampling and data-gathering techniques to increase reliability and generalizability. Thus, this study had a strong review of literature and could have improved sampling and data-gathering techniques.

References

American Psychological Association (2001). *Publication Manual of the American Psychological Association* (5th). Washington, DC: American Psychological Association.

Frey, L. R., Botan, C. H., & Kreps, G. L. (2000). *Investigating communication: An introduction to research methods* (2nd). Needham Heights, MA: Allyn and Bacon.

Honeycutt, J. M., & Wiemann, J. M. (1999). Analysis of functions of talk and reports of imagined interactions (IIs) during engagement and marriage. *Human Communication Research, 25,* 399-420.

Sparks, L. (2005). [Personal communication] *Introduction to Research Methods Lecture.* George Mason University, Fairfax, VA.